HARVARD CO–OPERATIVE SOCIETY

LONDON : HUMPHREY MILFORD
OXFORD UNIVERSITY PRESS

FRONT OF THE MAIN STORE, 1942

Harvard Co-operative Society
Past and Present
1882-1942

BY

N. S. B. GRAS

STRAUS PROFESSOR OF BUSINESS HISTORY
GRADUATE SCHOOL OF BUSINESS ADMINISTRATION
HARVARD UNIVERSITY

HARVARD UNIVERSITY PRESS
CAMBRIDGE, MASSACHUSETTS
1942

PRINTED AT THE HARVARD UNIVERSITY PRINTING OFFICE
CAMBRIDGE, MASS., U.S.A.

PREFACE

THIS history of the Harvard Co-operative Society was undertaken simply to make known the facts to the officers, directors, and members of the Society, to the many former members, and to the outside public. What appeared at first to be a simple job of unfolding small events has proved to be a highly intricate task of interpreting and appraising policies and procedures. The reader will not go far without discovering that it was individual men and groups of men and not cosmic, or even national, forces that worked creatively. He will learn that after twenty years of idealism there followed forty years of success.

In this age of strange book titles, I thought of the following possibilities.

So this is the Coop	Have you a Number, Sir?
I got it at the Coop	Adventure in College Co-oper-
Meet me at the Coop	ation
Pardon my Business Style	

My mid-Victorian preference at least insures the book against being a best seller.

The preliminary work of putting together the pertinent material in the office of the secretary of the Society, in the Widener and Baker Libraries, and in the Library of the Massachusetts Institute of Technology has been done by Miss Evelyn H. Puffer (Mrs. Harry E. Knowlton). She compiled a great many statistical tables, all of which have been used and a few of which have been drawn upon for reproduction in the statistical appendices, and a great many graphs, for none of which was there room in this small volume. Among the sources copiously used are the following: Minutes of the Directors, newspapers (especially the *Crimson*), operational statistics from the controller's office, Cases compiled at the School of Business (and duly released for the purpose of this study), and Reports to the Harvard Bureau of Business Research (also duly released).

Many persons (over 250) have answered my letters of inquiry. It is best that I leave them unnamed, but I am grateful to them individually and collectively. All of the present officers and directors of the Society approached have courteously answered my questions. Over a dozen employees have discussed the affairs of the Society's three stores, some frankly, some guardedly. I have also consulted former employees and present customers.

The excellent secretary of the Society, Mr. Walter Humphreys, has encouraged the writing of this history from the very first, as has the president, Mr. Henry S. Thompson. Mr. Humphreys facilitated the use of the records in his office and has drawn upon his wide fund of information to help me piece together the facts of various situations.

Professor Austin W. Scott, vice-president of the Society, has given generously of his time in reviewing this history. His criticisms have been keen and incisive. In general, they have provided a much-needed institutional point of view to counterbalance my own more individualistic approach.

When I entered the office of the manager — it must have been very early in 1941 — in search of information about the history of the Society, I did not realize that there had already been something of a demand elsewhere for such a history. Mr. Cole, with the best spirit of a business man, saw in me the supply. Because of the fact that a History of the Society entered Mr. Cole's consciousness so late, however, he had done very little in the past to facilitate the work, for instance, by way of preserving early operation records. From first to last, nevertheless, he has talked with me frankly, has given me all the material in his possession which I asked for, and has done innumerable small things which greatly relieved the burden on me.

From the first examination of the Society's records, to see whether there was material for a history, down to the reading of the finished manuscript, I have had the benefit of the assistance and criticism of my colleague, Dr. Henrietta M. Larson, associate professor of Business History at the Harvard School of Business. I have consulted Professor Malcolm P. McNair on a few but very important matters and always received (and followed) his friendly advice.

Professor Wallace B. Donham, formerly dean of the School of Business, and Mr. Donald K. David, the present dean, have encouraged me in the writing of this history and in fact made the work possible. They have themselves both played important parts in the administration of the Harvard Co-operative Society.

Mrs. Elsie H. Bishop has read all the manuscript, read the proof, and made the index. Her advice, based on good judgment and long experience, has been invaluable. To Miss Madeleine A. Cummings, my best thanks are due for the hurried examination of sundry scattered materials not directly available to me.

My wife has been compiler, typist, adviser, and critic. Without her assistance the work would not have been undertaken or, if undertaken, not completed in any reasonable period.

I have asked four specially qualified officers and directors of the Society to read the manuscript in the interest of accuracy, propriety, and utility. I have gained immeasurably from their knowledge and experience and perhaps have erred in not always following their advice. This work is not an official history: I alone am responsible for facts and opinions.

My reward for writing this history has been in part the chance to learn something from life as well as from documents and in part the receipt of free copies for distribution among the members of the Business Historical Society.

N. S. B. GRAS

19 July, 1942

CONTENTS

LIST OF ILLUSTRATIONS xiii

LIST OF GRAPHS xiv

CHAPTER I

FOUNDATION AND EARLY DIFFICULTIES, 1882–1890

§1. Mr. Kip invites the fellows in 3
§2. Students organize the Co-operative 6
§3. The store opens for business 9
§4. Good-by, Mr. Kip 13
§5. Ups and downs of business, 1882–1885 15
§6. A revolution in business policies, 1887 18
§7. Exit Mr. Waterman, 1890 23

CHAPTER II

PROBLEM OF CONTROLLING THE SUPERINTENDENT, 1890–1899

§1. Prosperity of the Society 27
§2. Factors in prosperity 28
§3. Departments in the store — goods and services provided by the
  Society 31
§4. Difficulties of controlling management 33
§5. Financial and cost accounting 34
§6. The second superintendent is dropped, 1899 40

CHAPTER III

LAYING NEW FOUNDATIONS, 1899–1906

§1. The Medical Branch manager in charge, 1899–1903 . . . 44
§2. The need for reorganization, 1892–1902 47
§3. Incorporation and trusteeship, 1902–1903 50
§4. A new superintendent and a new building, 1903–1906 . . . 53
§5. The new foundation stones, 1899–1906 58

CHAPTER IV

GROWTH AND STRONG ADMINISTRATION, 1906–1919
THE PRESIDENT PLANS AND CONTROLS

§1. Professor Munro takes the president's chair 61
§2. Superintendents follow fast, 1911–1915 70
§3. The Co-operative branches out 72
§4. The Technology Store 73
§5. Just mishaps 77
§6. Results of operation, 1906–1919 80

CHAPTER V

PROSPERITY AND STABILITY, 1919–1942
THE MANAGER STEERS THE SHIP

§1. George E. Cole — the man and the manager 84
§2. Stability through long service 86
§3. The decemvirate — the (board of) stockholders 89
§4. Prosperity, 1919–1942 92
§5. The Main Store in the new building, 1925 — present . . . 94
§6. The Technology Store, 1937 — present 97
§7. School of Business Store in crowded seclusion 99
§8. Employees who left for fame or stayed at hame 102
§9. Managerial changes and results, 1919–1942 106
§10. President Henry S. Thompson: financial strength 115
§11. Problems ahead of the Society 119

CHAPTER VI

SERVICES — PAST AND PRESENT

§1. Influence on other college co-operatives 125
§2. Goods and services abandoned or lost 130
§3. Special services — paid for and free 131
§4. Service through the sale of goods 133
§5. Prices and dividends 134
§6. Education in co-operation and in business 136

QUESTIONS AND ANSWERS 139

APPENDICES 143
1. Presidents, 1882–1942 145
2. Vice-presidents, 1919–1942 145
3. Secretaries, 1882–1942 145
4. Treasurers, 1882–1942 146
5. Superintendents, 1882–1942 146
6. Directors, 1882–1942 147
7. Stockholders, 1902–1942 149
8. Broad Classification of Membership, 1882–1942 151
9. Operation and Finances, 1882–1942 153
10. Expenses and Profits and also Balance Available for Dividends
    and Surplus as Percentages of Sales, 1882–1941 . . . 156
11. Break-down of Expenses (1) by Functions and (2) by Natural
    Divisions, in Percentages of Sales, 1926–1940 158
12. Rate of Dividends, 1897–1942 159
13. Analysis of Sales (Cash, Charge, Installment) in the Three
    Stores, 1923–1941 160
14. Number of Members Classified according to the Amount of
    their Annual Purchases (Every Fifth Year from 1924–25) 164
15. Number of Employees by Divisions and Departments, 1922–
    1942 165
16. Number of Employees and their Performance, 1926–1940 . . 166
17. Pay-Roll Expenses as Percentages of Sales, 1924–1940 . . 167
18. Constitution and By-laws of the Association (Unlimited Part-
    nership), 1900 168
19. By-laws of the Corporation, as Revised, 1903–1942 . . . 171

INDEX 181

LIST OF ILLUSTRATIONS

1. Front of the Main Store, 1942. Pen drawing made by Marguerite Poté Hanlon (Mrs. Gordon B. Hanlon) . . . . *frontispiece*

2. Charles Hayden Kip about 1882, Founder of the Society. Reproduction of a photograph, Pach Bros., New York, in Widener Archives 4

3. Professor James B. Ames in 1885, Savior of the Society. Reproduction of a photograph, J. Notman, Boston, in Widener Archives 16

4. Dane Hall about 1890, the Society's Third Home, 1883–1903. Reproduction of a photograph in the Widener Collection . . 32

5. Professor Frank W. Taussig in 1901, President 1890–94, 1895–96. Reproduction of a photograph, Pach Bros., New York, in Widener Archives 38

6. Lyceum Hall in 1908, the Society's Fourth Home, 1903–24. Reproduction of part of a photograph, made with the permission of Miss Marie Louise Olsson, J. F. Olsson and Company, Cambridge 56

7. William Bennett Munro about 1930, President 1906–18, 1919–22. Reproduction of a photograph, made with the permission of the Maryland Studio, Pasadena 62

8. George E. Cole in 1942, Superintendent 1915–19, manager since 1919. Reproduction of a photograph, made with the permission of the Marshall Studio, Cambridge 84

9. Main Floor in the Main Store, 1942. Reproduction of a photograph, made with the permission of the Fellman Studio, Malden, Mass. 94

10. New Technology Store, 1937. Reproduction of a photograph, made with the permission of Paul J. Weber, Boston . . . 96

11. Technology Store, Main Floor, 1937. Reproduction of a photograph, made with the permission of Paul J. Weber, Boston . 98

12. Technology Store, Luncheonette, 1937. Reproduction of a photograph, made with the permission of Paul J. Weber, Boston . 99

13. Henry S. Thompson, President since 1922. Reproduction of a photograph, made with the permission of Bachrach, Boston 116

14. Book Department, Main Store, 1942. Reproduction of a photograph, made with the permission of the Fellman Studio, Malden, Mass. 132

LIST OF GRAPHS

Structural Analysis of the Co-operative 64
Classification of Customers 110
Business Régimes Exemplified by the Society's Growth . . . 118
Classes of "Members" 122
Possible Genesis of College Co-operatives 125

HARVARD CO–OPERATIVE SOCIETY

CHAPTER I

FOUNDATION AND EARLY DIFFICULTIES
1882–1890

§1. Mr. Kip invites the fellows in. It was Charles Hayden Kip, of Buffalo, New York, who invited his fellow students at Harvard College to come to his room to discuss the formation of a co-operative society. Kip occupied room 24 in Holworthy Hall, and 41 of the 42 invited were said by him to have arrived. Although the room was large, the presence of so many persons must have presented a problem to hospitality. On that day — February 22, 1882 — discussion of the plan was entirely favorable, individual students making suggestions as to what might be done. The result was that a committee of five persons was appointed to take the next steps.

Mr. Kip was a junior at the time and noted for his college activities. He was a member of the staff of the *Harvard Daily Echo*, in which an article had appeared on January 18, 1882, setting forth the evils of high prices and the need for reform. The article was pointed by the reflection that they did things rather better at Princeton. Mr. Kip was an ideal person to lead a movement. He was full of enthusiasm. He thought more of others than of himself. That he was not himself a poverty-stricken student, is indicated by a picture of his well-decorated room. He was a descendant of the old Dutch family that gave its name to Kip's Bay. He was a hammer- and discus-thrower, a shot-putter, an oarsman, and, it is said, a football player. Lest we may conclude that Mr. Kip was the only outstanding man at Harvard at the time, we may well stop to note that Eliot was president of the University and that he was already surrounded by many able scholars, including James Russell Lowell, Charles Eliot Norton, Charles F. Dunbar, Christopher Columbus Langdell, and Justin Winsor.

In spite of the distinctions that were coming to Harvard, low cost of living was not one of them. Poor boys were continuing to attend Harvard and were encountering baffling difficulties in paying the tuition of $150 and meeting the expense of room, board, fuel, books, and clothing. Even the cost of blue books was a serious item, for in those days students had to provide the books on the occasion of examinations.

Whether the students of that time were more active than those of recent years is hard to say. Certainly, they were doing a lot of extra-curricular things. They were managing, or mismanaging, the Memorial Hall Dining Association. They had started the *Crimson* in 1873, the *Lampoon* in 1876, the *Echo* in 1879, and the *Herald* in 1882. All of these, and the *Advocate* in addition, favored action in reducing the cost of living at Harvard Square.

The Harvard students were united in believing that prices at Harvard Square were outrageous and that students were the most oppressed group in the world. Many felt keenly the position they were in; only a few stopped to reflect upon the reason for high prices at Harvard Square and even they did not uncover the whole situation. There seem to have been at least three parts to the bad economic position at the Square. First, many students bought goods on credit and some did not pay their bills. One student in 1882 is credited with a debit of 22 suits, in this case in Boston. One tailor tried to collect for three suits but found that the student was a minor and desisted. If the student lived in another State, legal action would have been unpromising. Some of the faculty members who bought groceries and other goods at local stores paid only periodically or when their bills had reached large proportions. In other words, prices had to be high to cover inefficient and dishonest dealing. Second, there was a good deal of careless ordering. Many individuals bought goods without asking the price. There has been a hang-over in America of the European aristocratic contempt for prices and costs. This bad buying habit was an invitation to the tradesman to get the most. Third, there was for many

CHARLES HAYDEN KIP ABOUT 1882, FOUNDER OF THE SOCIETY

commodities something like a monopoly at the Square. True, students could go elsewhere but much time would be used up. There was the Union Railroad Company that operated street-cars (horsecars in 1882) between Harvard Square and Boston via three routes — (1) Main Street, (2) Broadway and East Cambridge, and (3) between the Square and Cambridgeport via Prospect Street. In practice, students provided for most of their needs right at the Square.

Clearly, it is one thing to complain of high prices and another to take action against them, as the students themselves observed in 1882. There had been several, two recorded, instances of individual students organizing the buying needs of their fellows, particularly for books, and circumventing booksellers at the Square. The new plan, however, was to form a business unit that would provide several kinds of goods and services and continue in business. The particular form of unit decided upon was co-operative. Since this was the first instance of a co-operative store in an American college (so far as I know), we may well stop to inquire whence came the idea.

Mr. Kip said later in life that the idea of co-operation was born in the local situation of high prices; and that he had been turning it over in his mind as early as the autumn of 1881. Actually, the high prices created only the demand for a solution. Whence came the supply — the solution itself? The fame of British efforts — particularly the Rochdale stores — may have spread to Harvard. Holyoake's *History of Co-operation*, published in London, 1875–79, may have been read by students or instructors and its contents discussed. At least by April, 1882, a co-operative plan in effect at the University of Toronto was being discussed at Harvard. Of this Canadian effort, however, I have found no other trace.

The hard times in America, particularly since 1873, had drained the resources of the parents of many of the students. While the parents of the students had a diminished income, owing partly to receding prices (1866–97), their sons at Harvard suffered from continuing high prices. Here and there in

America, co-operative ventures had been suggested and undertaken as a way out of such difficulties. What Mr. Kip did was to suggest and to start such a venture at Harvard.

§2. Students organize the Co-operative. The committee of five students prepared a constitution as directed, and without delay. This constitution was presented on February 28, 1882, and voted upon at a general meeting. It was not to go into effect until 400 persons, connected with Harvard, had subscribed to it.

This original constitution, made up of 13 clauses, was really a mixture of fundamental items and by-laws. By 1893 the two categories had been separated. The most important clauses of 1882 set forth the following points. A membership fee of two dollars should be paid and should apply to the academic year in which it was paid. This soon proved embarrassing, particularly in the case of seniors whose college career would be over in about three or four months. A board of directors, a president, and a treasurer were provided for, the two officers to be chosen by the Society at large. Although no secretary was mentioned, one was soon selected, and the office became important and has remained so throughout the Society's history. The board of directors was given the right to draw up all necessary rules and to manage the Society. It was to appoint a superintendent (general manager) who was to be charged with buying and selling and keeping accounts, the latter to be audited thrice yearly (not at that time by a public accountant). The board of directors might appoint assistants to the superintendent.

The constitution of 1882 envisaged three principal sources of income — membership dues, commissions on second-hand goods sold for members, and profits (not over 5 per cent) on other goods sold. The surplus at the end of each year was to be added to the capital. Any deficit was to be made up by a levy on members. This was to become an important assurance to creditors, for many of the members were of well-to-do families. Nonmembers had no rights but might buy second-hand stuff left by members for sale. All general transactions were to be for cash. If the Society should experience difficulty in purchasing large quantities of materials, for example fuel, the treasurer was authorized to ask the Harvard Corporation to guarantee the payment. The duty of "the faculty member" (sic) was stated to be the procuring of lists of textbooks to be used in classes; and, indeed, rival retailers were to complain of this practice as a vicious monopoly. Since Professor Lanman of the Sanskrit Department was the first faculty member, he must have been the original abettor of the "monopoly." All unspecified powers of administration were vested in the board of directors. Amendments might be made by the officers and directors, but these were not valid after the next general meeting of the Society, unless ratified.

At least three of the policies set forth in this constitution are noteworthy, for on them depended in large part the success that followed. The first of these is that sales should be for cash. This at once struck a blow at the expensive buying habits of the university community. The second is that profits should be added to capital. Thus, there was no specific provision for dividends on members' purchases. The advantages to the members lay in the chance to buy goods at not over 5 per cent above cost, to employ the Society to handle their cast-off furniture and unneeded books, and so on. Nevertheless, dividends actually came to be paid after five years of struggling existence. The third provision of note is that a superintendent was to be appointed. Previous discussion had envisaged the employment of from three to five undergraduates who were thought of as enjoying scholarships under this plan. From this arrangement escape was providential.

Who was chiefly instrumental in drawing up this constitution is unknown to me. Probably the chief formulator was the Law School student, Frank Bolles, who became the first president of the Society. Mr. Kip's chief interest is said to have been a co-operative coal yard. Josiah Quincy ('80) is said to have suggested the plan of buying from affiliated retailers. Perhaps Bolles helped to consolidate and formulate. It was decided that the number of directors was to be fifteen (later reduced), two of whom were to represent the Law School and one each class and each faculty, including those of the Divinity School and the Episcopal Theological Seminary. It was true at the beginning, as it was up to 1906 (or even to the present time), that the Law School played a strong rôle in the history of the Society.

Mr. Kip was asked not long before his death why he had not become president. His reply was that *his* job was to boost the Society, particularly to persuade tradesmen to give discounts to its members. Certainly, his group on the *Echo* were the earliest supporters, for three out of the five who drew up the constitution were on the editorial board of that daily paper. There was plenty of boosting to do and all of the college papers participated. The *Crimson* was not far behind the *Echo* but it was more critical. The big job was to get students to sign up. By March 15, 1882, the necessary 400 had subscribed. There was a vast difference, however, between subscribing to the constitution and paying for membership. By May 10 only 250 had actually paid their dues, but by September 30 the number was 500.

The original list of members has apparently been lost, but A. A. Waterman, the first superintendent, held ticket number one. These ticket-holders were the original "stockholders" — the investing capitalists — who put in their $2.00 apiece to help a venture that was to assist in reducing the cost of living at Harvard. The investment of each was small and in practice it could never be taken out; and thus it has continued to this day. After some changes, the amount was fixed in 1893 at only $1.00 a year. At this figure it has remained with very little challenge, except from those who would abolish the fee system entirely, as has been done in some other college co-operatives.

Because of the fact that Frank Bolles was connected with the Society only one year, we could easily pass over his real importance in promoting, formulating, and administering it. Born in Winchester, Massachusetts, he was the son of a brigadier-general of the Civil War and of the sister of John A. Dix, governor of New York. He had lived in Baltimore and Washington and went to the Harvard Law School, having already obtained the degree of LL.B. at another institution. While a student at Harvard, he not only assisted Mr. Kip in launching the Harvard

Co-operative Society but helped to organize a club to lend furniture to poor students at moderate cost and planned a cooperative dormitory. Thus we see that, if Mr. Kip had not suggested the Society, Frank Bolles might have done so. He was an editorial writer on the *Echo*, along with Mr. Kip, and also advertising manager. He is said to have taken over the entire management of the paper and made it profitable. In 1883 he became editorial writer on the Boston *Advertiser*, and in 1886 private secretary to President Eliot and during the same year secretary of Harvard University. It was he who set up an employment bureau to assist students in getting jobs during the summer and on leaving college. Bolles was one of those who tried in many ways to help students in a period of hard times. Mr. Kip knew him for what he was and deliberately enlisted his support.

All the evidence indicates that the Society was devised by students and begun by them. They provided the ship, the navigator, the captain, and the crew. Whether any law professor or other faculty member stood by with friendly advice in navigation as the ship left the harbor is not known to me.

Historians may be divided into two classes — the diffusionists and the effusionists. Those who belong to the well-filled ranks of the first group will probably look to some institution out of which the Harvard Co-operative Society grew, for they cannot conceive an original birth. They will perhaps be comforted with the possibility that it was the *Harvard Daily Echo* (1879–82) that fathered the Society. In a sense that is true. On the other hand, the scant band of effusionists will say that it was Kip and Bolles and Quincy who sought in their own way to solve the problems of hard-pressed students struggling along at what was called "the most expensive university in America" and at a time when the long downtrend in business was depleting their family fortunes.

§3. The store opens for business. It was about March 20, 1882, that the Harvard Co-operative Society opened its store for business. The location was at 13 Harvard Row, or what is now the store next to Church Street, in the old College House on Massachusetts Avenue. The undertaking did not occupy the whole store but rather a shelf or two in what was chiefly a fruit store.

When the promoters of the Society looked around for a location for their new enterprise, they hit upon the already going concern of Arthur A. Waterman of the class of 1885. Indeed, it is said that they finally chose as director a classmate and friend of Waterman so as to win his consent to come into the venture. Clearly, Waterman was recognized as the man for the job — the man who was to translate into realities the dreams of Kip and the constitutional clauses of Bolles. Waterman came from Chatauqua County in Western New York, indeed not so far from Kip's home town of Buffalo. He had taught school in Iowa in order to be able to attend Harvard College, but apparently he was still short of cash and was therefore engaged in a little business of his own at the same time that he attempted to meet the scholastic requirements of the College.

Waterman had set up retailing on a five-foot shelf containing stationery and some second-hand books belonging to a fellow-student. He was persuaded to transfer his stock to the newly formed Co-operative Society and to be its first manager. He was given the title of assistant superintendent at first but was soon promoted to be superintendent. Before long, his salary was $1,200 a year and apparently he was never required to devote all his time to the Society. Soon we find him and a fellow student acting as ticket brokers for trips westward via the Hoosac Tunnel! The business ventures soon ate in upon academic ambition, and the prospects of a degree were abandoned. Fifty years later the class of 1885 honored Waterman for his work on behalf of its members.

Clearly, it was Waterman or nobody, and Waterman justified the confidence placed in him. He was resourceful and enthusiastic. He persuaded others that a co-operative society could work and he demonstrated to other business men that he would keep his word and meet all obligations. Bookstores and janitors were against him and critics scoffed. When the boys came in, they said, "So this is the Coop." Whereupon Waterman would stand erect with the rejoinder, "Yes, this is the Harvard Co-operative Society."

The location in College House was not ideal. Not enough student traffic centered there. After about one month, the store was moved to Drury's tobacco shop in Holyoke House, where boys came for cigars and cigarettes, smoking tobacco, meerschaum pipes, and the like. There, in the back part of the store, the members could find a competent assistant to show them stationery and books between the hours of 8 A.M. and 8:30 P.M., except for an hour and a quarter at noon.

The Co-operative Society has always had the capacity for doing new things. After nearly 18 months' stay at Drury's tobacco store, it moved (October, 1883) across the road to Dane Hall, the old Law School building that had been built in 1832 (now replaced by Lehman Hall). Here there was a chance to expand, and here the students could buy their supplies without leaving the Yard. The University may have been persuaded to make this arrangement by the second president of the Society, John W. White, professor of Greek, or by the third president, Charles S. Lanman, professor of Sanskrit. Beginning in 1886, the Society became a paying guest while at Dane Hall. Since it remained here 21 years, the rental was probably regarded as favorable.

A store is what a store does, not what its sponsors have planned. Let us see what kind of business was actually done during the second month of existence. We may consider six main categories:

(1) Sale of goods on hand — blue books (2 or 3 cents), notebooks (two-thirds the usual price), stylographic (fountain-pen) ink, stationery (at one third to one-half off the usual price).

(2) Sale by order — books (10 to 33% discount), periodicals, and tennis equipment ($5.00 rackets for $3.75, if 12 persons left orders).

(3) Purchase at affiliated stores — 30 firms listed, the saving being from 5 to 33 per cent (discount justified because all sales were for cash).

(4) Orders for coal and wood. The coal was to be provided by a Boston firm at a saving of 30 cents a ton on anthracite and $1.00 on soft coal (instead of an earlier expectation of saving $2.00 a ton on "coal").

(5) Sale of furniture and second-hand books for members at a commission.

(6) Storage of furniture against the owner's return in September (free, if the furniture had been bought through the Society). The Old Gymnasium was available for storage purposes.

The only capital tied up was invested in the small stock of goods on hand. This was doubtless covered by the fee of $2.00 from each of the 400-odd paid-up members. The rest of the work was on a commission basis. The chief expenses were the salary of the superintendent, the wages of an assistant, and the rental for the part of the store used. It was early recognized that this very conservative beginning might really prove to be a weakness because no one would lose very much if the venture fell through. There was one person who stood a chance to lose, however, that is, Waterman, the superintendent, who was coming to look upon business rather than education as his chief concern at Harvard. True, he struggled along for four years in the College and the Law School but without taking a degree. Some of his very good friends — freshmen — helped him to keep the Society going. After all, they would have the greatest stake in the venture — over three years of trading.

An examination of the rather full report of the treasurer at the end of the first fiscal year (after actual operation of eleven months) shows that cash receipts had amounted to $14,764, and that the net balance or "true capital" remaining in goods, fixtures, and money was $364. An estimated saving to the members was put at $4,500. Thus, the total financial advantage of operation was $4,864. Deduct from this $1,163 paid as fees and you have a net gain of $3,701 for the first year's operation. Beyond this was some really valuable training in business methods. And also, we should not forget the lowered prices at the three rival bookstores, enjoyed by members and non-members alike.

Let us recall again the fact that it was the students, not the faculty, that planned, organized, and administered the Society during the first year. By February, 1883, there were 699 student members as against 14 faculty members. About 49 per cent of the student body had signed up, while only 8.6 per cent of the faculty had joined. Efforts were made by Professor White, the second president, to enroll instructors in the Society by arranging (1883–84) for the co-operative purchase of groceries. Only limited results followed. Whether the faculty was just apathetic, or shied away from the financial responsibility involved in a possible levy to meet a deficit, is not clear.

§4. Good-by, Mr. Kip. The summer of 1883 saw Mr. Kip leave college with his class. He had been re-elected as secretary of the Co-operative Society, but did not serve. Indeed, I can find no evidence of any subsequent connection with the Society.

Mr. Kip seems to have spent the years 1883–1925 in business in Boston. First, he was in the employ of the Boston and Albany Railroad; later, he was in manufacturing; and, finally, he was a security salesman for various investment houses.

It was really the activities of Mr. Kip outside business that brought him distinction. He was a member of the Boston City Democratic Committee and of the Boston School Committee. He organized boys' camps and became a leader of the Boy Scouts, both locally and nationally. For thirty years he was a scoutmaster of a Brookline troop. Here we see the undergraduate of 1879–83 still seeking to help others.

In May, 1941, my colleague, Dr. Henrietta M. Larson, visited Mr. Kip and left her notes with me. Somewhat shortened, they run as follows.

Mr. Kip was a tall, slender, stooped old man, with an intelligent and kindly face; he was nearly blind, and somewhat shabby in dress. He lived in a wing of an old house that was drab outside and dark inside. Books and papers were scattered about his rooms in process of being sorted with the idea of disposing of them.

I introduced myself by telling of the study in process of the Harvard Co-operative Society. Mr. Kip expressed great appreciation of my not saying "Coop." I said I understood that he had taken a leading part in the beginnings of the Co-operative. Would he tell me just what he had done?

Mr. Kip said that he had had the idea originally and talked it over with some of the boys. Then he made up a plan for an organization and got a large number of students and instructors together in his room and thus had been instrumental in getting the Co-operative started.

Asked whether he had been interested in the co-operative movement as such, Mr. Kip said he had not, but he had been impressed with the high charges of local "tradesmen," especially for coal and clothes. He smilingly said the Dutch in him may have had something to do with it. Since his father had plenty of money, the situation did not directly concern him, but he was much concerned about the boys who had less money than he. He said that it was helping the other fellow that made the world go around. He had always felt that he should do what he could for others and he hated unfairness.

As I was about to leave, he asked whether I would do something for him. The girl who was helping him needed a job. She was a teacher and a splendid young lady. Would I inquire around to see whether I could help her secure a position? She was in need and very worthy. He would be very much pleased if I would keep her in mind.

I asked Mr. Kip whether he had any letters or other manuscript material that might give information concerning the beginnings of the Co-operative Society. He said he had no such records but that the best source was the *Echo*.

Mr. Kip, I felt, had diagnosed himself aright. Though the young man who had started the Co-operative sixty years ago was not the old man of today, a sense of responsibility for others and a love of fairness seemed to be fundamentals in his character. There was, moreover, in all that he said, in his clothes, and in his surroundings, evidence of that unconcern about oneself which often bespeaks a deep interest in one's fellow men. If one judged by clothes and surroundings, alone, one would say that he was a rather pathetic old man.

Mr. Kip died at the age of 81, on March 31, 1942. Not long previously he had gently declined an invitation to lunch with us at Harvard.

Good-by, Mr. Kip! Much good you have done to thousands of fellow students who have never known your name. Success came from your idea of co-operation but through a gradual reversal of much that you and the idealistic co-operative movement have stood for.

§5. Ups and downs of business, 1882–1885. The Co-operative Society did very well at the start. The first year's business amounted to $13,600, and the second to $18,230. A writer in the *Crimson* called the Society a "decided success." It had reduced the price of textbooks by from 5 to 15 per cent and law books by 10 per cent. Stylographic pens, usually priced at $2.00, were sold at $1.25. The sellers of second-hand furniture got more and the buyers paid less. In December, 1882, reduced rates by rail to points west had been arranged. Moreover, books were provided on time — when possible. One story is told about Dana's *Geology*. The instructor using this work as a text had informed the publisher and a local bookstore, but not the Co-operative, about the needs of his class. Here was a threatened black eye. Freshmen, however, solved the problem by going to the local book dealer, who was himself selling at reduced rates, and buying each a copy for himself and one for his roommate. Soon this storekeeper was sold out, but the Co-operative had copies, for the freshmen had turned over their second copies to it for resale. The day was saved. The freshmen had proved that their fellow-student Waterman was a good business man! Not least of the Co-operative's accomplishments, recognized at the time, was the forcing downward of prices of books at Charles W. Sever's University Bookstore and at Moses King's new bookstore. We are not sure at this distance just what to think of this result, for books were not profitable articles to handle even at the old prices.

One writer in the *Crimson* reported on the results of the second year's operations. He thought the year had been "moderately prosperous." It was expected that a net capital of about $100 would be forthcoming. It is true there had been a "slight abatement in the interest and support accorded to" the Cooperative Society, which had had to "run on a close financial basis." Obviously, it "would be much better if it had a small capital of its own."

During 1884 business turned for the worse at the Society's store, as it did in America generally. In the summer of 1884 a loan of $500 was secured from the Track Fund. By January, 1885, the worst was known. The surplus was then about $550, but the (estimated) deficit by September, 1885, would be about $400. This was threatening to the Society and alarming to its friends.

Officers and members looked about for an explanation. Waterman, the superintendent, was declared to be a man of zeal and integrity. No, it was the students who were to blame: they had not signed up in sufficiently large numbers and they had not made purchases as expected. In order to make up on fees, the rate was raised to $2.50 in September, 1884, and that probably deterred men from joining. One student member had been expelled from the Society for loaning his card to a fellow-student to use in making purchases. The second-hand furniture department was temporarily discontinued in May, 1884, though a book for registering furniture for sale was to be set up.

Two paragraphs from the *Crimson* of January 30, 1885, are worth quoting:

The why and wherefore of the present condition of the society is very simple. Last year extra service was hired, extra inducements offered, and the business of the society was enlarged generally. As a result, last year was the first really successful year of the society's existence. Basing their calculations on these results, the superintendent and directors decided on certain additions and enlargements in the business and work of the society, calculating on a membership of one thousand and five per ct. profit on transactions. But it turns out that they have a membership of only 790, with proportionately less

PROFESSOR JAMES B. AMES IN 1885, SAVIOR OF THE SOCIETY

transactions, and have retained but three and a half per cent. on the transactions. This, continued through the year, would leave the society with a deficit of about $1500. The whole machinery is at last in admirable working order, but it could just as well do three times the work it now does — and would need to do one-third more work in order to pay expenses without assessments.

The apathy of the students is not alone to blame, however. The memberships and transactions are not so large as they should be, and that is the great cause of failure, but at the same time the superintendent should not have sold things too cheap. If five per cent. profit was needed, five per cent. profit ought to have been made. And it is but a poor consolation that the money which should have gone to the supporting of the society went into the pockets of members buying goods.

I think that we may sum up the situation rather briefly. It had been assumed that the accelerating business of 1882–84 would be continued during 1884–85. A large stock ($35 worth of calendars still unsold, and $250 worth of soap on hand) had been purchased, and improvements in the arrangements of the store had been made. An unusually large staff had been provided. And, then, the familiar turn of the cycle occurred — familiar enough to business men but not at that time to students and professors. If the Society had possessed a capital of $2,000, there would have been little worry and less danger. If the superintendent had been conscious of the business cycle, the trouble would probably not have arisen.

President James B. Ames (of the Law School) expressed the opinion on January 21, 1885, that it would be better to discontinue the Society's operation. One week later, Dr. Frank W. Taussig (Political Economy) made the motion to close the store. On February 2, 1885, Ames made a decisive move. If the members would raise (not by assessment) the sum of $600, he would guarantee that the liabilities at the end of the academic year would be not over $200 and that the surplus of stock over liabilities would be not over $500. So then the cry was "$600 before Monday night." Finally, the sum of $551.50 was raised as a loan and that sum was accepted by Ames and the Society.

On February 16 the directors decided to continue operation. The crisis had passed. It was the small sum of $551.50 rather than the student body of 1,586 men that saved the day. This loan tided the Society over its worst year. We wonder why the Corporation of Harvard College did not come to the rescue. Of course, those were the days of *laissez-faire* — let come and let go. The Corporation had watched many a student affair blow in and blow out.

But we are now confronted with this question: what impelled the Harvard group to raise the amount in question in a year of business crisis? There are two considerations. First, there was the thought that prices would again go up if the Co-operative should die. Second, the College pride was aroused, and this came about in an interesting way. During the crucial days of January 21–February 16 it was reported that Yale had formed a co-operative society, that Amherst was agitating for one, and that a professor from the University of Michigan had come to see how success had been attained in Cambridge, so that he could take back good advice to the co-operative society newly formed at Ann Arbor. All this was just too much for local pride. At least this pride rose to the height of $551.50, though it refused to go to $600.

§6. A revolution in business policies, 1887. The year 1884–85, as we have seen, threatened to end in a loss, which precipitated the whole question of dissolution. The year 1885–86 is almost a blank in the Minutes of the Directors: it seems to have witnessed the highest volume of sales up to date, namely $27,000. At the meeting of November 15, 1886, the directors authorized the president to act as trustee in investing $1,500 of the Society's funds. Probably much of this amount arose from autumn sales of the year 1886 (September) to 1887 (September). Clearly, the Society was recovering, as general business picked up in America as a whole.

Our interest at this point is directed away from the actual performance of business to the formulation of new policies. These were presented to the directors and by them discussed on

April 26, 1887. Then, at a general meeting of about 50 members, the new policies were accepted to take effect September, 1887. Those fifty-odd men did a good job, even if they only accepted the wisdom of their leaders.

The first innovation was to throw open the ordering and purchasing of goods to all members of Harvard, the Annex (Radcliffe), and the Episcopal Theological Seminary, whether those persons were members of the Co-operative or not. Thus, the store was no longer so exclusive a place in which to deal. The number of potential customers was at one stroke greatly increased. A large number of persons (the ticket-holders or members of the Society) were carrying on a business in which an ever larger number of persons might participate. The alleged reason for taking the step in 1887 was "to increase the capital" of the Society. The reasoning was presumably that the net profits would be larger under this system and that therefore there would be a greater residue for the Society after dividends had been paid.

Perhaps at this point we should note a far-reaching implication of the extension of the right to buy to all connected with Harvard, Radcliffe, and the Episcopal Theological Seminary. To be sure, right at the beginning, non-members might buy second-hand goods left by members for the Society to sell on commission. It would seem that the decision to permit all connected with the three colleges to make purchases, whether they were members or not, was gradually to mean that anyone might come in and buy. As long as the Society's store was located in Dane Hall (on College premises), doubtless all or almost all customers were actually connected with the colleges. When the Society moved to its present site, however, the number of non-collegiate customers probably grew considerably. It never was practical to require a person connected with the colleges to present his credentials just to make a purchase. Hence the opening to the public. Beginning in 1929, a special effort was made to attract non-member customers. It would be good business policy now to give to each non-member (who buys goods) cash-register tickets which he could save and at the end of the financial year present to the Society as evidence of a claim to a dividend of, say, half the regular rate.

Prices came in for attention back in 1887 as now. The new plan was to raise the general level of prices of goods sold in the store but still to keep them below "ordinary retail prices," presumably lower than prices at other Harvard Square stores. On the other hand, the price of books was not to be raised but actually lowered "to any extent required to hold the business of the Society." In other words, stationery, sporting goods, probably men's furnishings, and so on, were to carry the book department.

The handling of books, particularly textbooks, had constituted a first-class problem for the Society right from the first. Now a definite policy was breaking through, particularly the work, I suspect, of Professors Ames and Taussig. In their letter of June 6, 1887, sent to instructors, we find some important points made. The Society was at last to deal with all members of Harvard University and not with just those who had joined the Society. It was to print and sell abstracts used in many courses in the University. It was to import all foreign books used. Above all, it was to have a monopoly of handling all textbooks.

> The Society will undertake to procure at its own risk the number of books which any instructor thinks needed for his courses for the ensuing academic year, provided that the instructor will give the Society exclusive information as to the books he will use. A monopoly is obviously necessary to warrant the Society in assuming an engagement of this kind.

But the professor of Law and the professor of Political Economy were planning a good "monopoly." "The Society intends to sell textbooks at the smallest profits possible, making, in this case, an exception from its regular business." The monopoly was to be good but imperfect, for, in case an instructor did *not* give the Society exclusive advance notice, the Society would take the students' orders for copies or would buy for chance sale such copies as it thought it could dispose of.

Dues were to be reduced to $1.50 a year. The history of these dues seems to be as follows:

| 1882–84 | — $2.00 | 1887–93 | — $1.50 |
| 1884–87 | — 2.50 | 1893–present | — 1.00 |

During the early years, bargain rates were offered for fractional parts of the college year.

The division of net profits among members was to be "in the proportion which the gross profit made on each member's transactions bears to the total gross profits on the transactions of all the members." In other words, only the profits on members' purchases were theoretically to be divided, the profits on non-members' purchases being added to capital and surplus. Earlier, there had been a proposal to sell at net cost and charge higher dues, thereby leaving no surplus. Now, on the contrary, provision was made for dividends and something over for capital and surplus. A little later, on November 21, 1888, a rule was made that approximately two-thirds of net profits should go to dividends and one-third to capital and surplus. This was roughly followed till 1903, when the purchase of a new store building had to be financed out of earnings.

The exclusive, financially profitable rights of members of the Society were henceforth two-fold — to share in the dividends and to purchase goods from affiliated tradesmen. Unfortunately, we have no statistics as to the volume of purchases from affiliated tradesmen — in early days at a discount for cash. We do have figures for dividends, however, from the year 1887–88 to the present, though a few of the annual amounts are uncertain. These figures will be found among the statistical appendices printed at the end of the present volume.

Now, the question arises as to the inspiration for the new policies. Be it noted that they were developed at a time of increasing business. There can be little question that the explanation lies not in what took place currently in 1887–88 but what had occurred back in 1884–85. At that time the directors and the president had been ready to close the Society. Pride ruled their wills, and they found ways of avoiding closing. The next task was to discover policies that would prevent disaster in the future. When the new policies were announced, they were declared to be similar to the plan of "the famous Rochdale Pioneers." At last, the executives of the Co-operative were deigning to learn from the greater experience of foreign co-operators.

It was explicitly stated, though not officially recorded, that the new policies were Waterman's suggestions. Elsewhere it was implied that the success of the Society under Ames (1884–90) resulted from his direction of affairs. The Minutes of the Directors, however, indicate a certain activity on Taussig's part that points to his initiative. Taussig's *Principles of Economics*, written much later, to be sure, indicates a familiarity with the experience and policies of the Rochdale Pioneers. But, in truth, it is quite likely that Taussig, Ames, and Waterman were jointly contributing to the new order in the affairs of the Society.

In spite of the promising new policies, there were still problems to be overcome. The Society found difficulty in purchasing books from certain publishers. Apparently, the private book-sellers at Harvard Square had secured outside assistance in combating the Co-operative. On March 2, 1888, the Society agreed to buy books from Amee and Waterman, Booksellers, the contract to be terminated on short notice in case the publishers recognized the Society and allowed the regular discounts. On March 14, 1889, there was an agreement with Messrs. A. A. Waterman and Company (apparently the Boston firm) whereby the latter would turn over books to them, presumably for resale. In both cases, the intermediary seems to have been set up for the occasion; and, in both cases, the superintendent, Waterman, seems to have been the central figure in circumventing the opposition of the publishers. So appreciative were the directors of the Society that on June 20, 1889, they decided to give Waterman a bonus, in addition to his salary of $1,200 a year. After $500 had been set aside for addition to capital and surplus, the rest was to be divided equally between Waterman and the members of the Society. This is an early instance of profit-sharing in the Society's affairs.

§7. Exit Mr. Waterman, 1890. The prosperity of the Society during the period 1882–90, except for 1884–85 and 1889–90, was considerable and was commonly ascribed to the abilities of the superintendent, Waterman. Sales went ahead, dividends were paid to members, and additions were made to capital and surplus. When the nation-wide depression of 1884–85 came along, Waterman received and deserved some of the blame for the difficulties experienced by the Society. Since there was nation-wide *prosperity* in 1889–90, there could be even more logic in finding fault with the superintendent.

Before looking into the question of Waterman's responsibility for the recession in the store's business, especially in 1889–90, let us consider the control exercised by the officers and directors of the Society, particularly during the presidency of Professor Ames. We find the officers and directors questioning the superintendent periodically, and even, on one occasion, asking for monthly reports. The superintendent thought the best he could do was to report twice a year. There were special committees appointed to look into various matters, for example, furniture (1883) and affiliated tradesmen (1890), but the nominating committee was the most active body of the kind! The president and the treasurers were active personally but only intermittently. The treasurers in this early period were very ineffective in checking the superintendent, because, whether students or instructors, they had little time to give to the job and were quite untrained for the work. This condition prevailed until the present century.

I get the feeling, as I go through the Minutes of the Directors and through the files of the *Crimson*, that one man was growing strong in the affairs of the Society. This was Dr. Frank W. Taussig, who had become instructor in Political Economy the year the Society was formed; and one year later he became a director of the Society. During the administration of President

Ames, Taussig grew in stature until he appeared to be the key man. This strength was recognized in 1890 by his election as president. Apparently as Ames' interest lagged, that of Taussig grew. As we have seen, he was probably largely instrumental in putting through the revolutionary policies of 1887. Following this, he seems to have made greater effort to control management. And, then, as Ames was ready to step out, he apparently became responsible for the ruling that capital should be double the current liabilities (January 15, 1890). The idea underlying this policy was that there should be no repetition of the near-disaster of the year 1884–85, such as again seemed imminent in this very year 1889–90.

As the reality of the Society's recession in 1889–90 became apparent, so did complaints arise as to the management of affairs by the superintendent. Issues of the *Crimson* on January 8 and 9, 1890, contained criticisms of the superintendent, Waterman. One statement was that numerous complaints had been made of the inadequacy of the store. It was said by way of illustration that the book and stationery departments had small stocks of goods and that even they were inferior. The clerks were said to have little acquaintance with the stock. It was said that there were many mistakes in the ordering of books and that there were delays in getting them, and that often the Boston and Cambridge private stores had supplies on hand days before the Co-operative received its quota. Mistakes in rendering bills to members had become annoying. The wood ordered through the Co-operative was said to be of poor quality. The old discount on coal and laundry had gone. In short, the *Crimson* charged that "the society appears to have been badly managed and to be sadly in need of reform."

The complainants were not slow in explaining how the mismanagement had arisen. They said that the superintendent was giving most of his time to his other interests, particularly his store in Boston. One statement was made to the effect that he was in the Society's office only two hours during the week. Certainly, the Society's agreement with Waterman was vague as to the amount of his time that was expected. The accusation was made that he had drained off the best assistants from the Society's store to his own in Boston and that he diverted the Society's business to his own store. President Ames made it clear that neither of these charges was true. In fact, I believe that the store of Waterman was set up at least in part to supply the Society with books which publishers had refused to provide.

Waterman comes close to being the one person who, more than any other, established the Society. He had enthusiasm, persistence, ingenuity, persuasiveness, and devotion to his work. He wanted the store to succeed. He could buy and sell goods. He could train and inspire his assistants. He could and did create the impression of strength and integrity in a business community that was wholly hostile. Those closest to Waterman knew these facts and they would endure much before impugning his conduct or questioning his motives. They knew he had often been ready to go down with the ship.

While Waterman could promote a business and manage many parts of it, in my opinion he could not grow with it beyond a certain point, nor could he create an accounting system that would tell the exact story. His books were in no condition in the year 1889–90 to be examined by an outside accountant. There was no doubt of his integrity, only a question of adequacy and accuracy. Waterman was one of the many millions of American business men who have been good petty capitalists but incapable of growing beyond a certain point. True, it may be that all he lacked was training in accounting, but I am inclined to think that he was temperamentally a promoter rather than a business manager. This view has been corroborated by a letter from Professor A. V. Woodworth, who was secretary of the Society, 1887–90.

During the first few months of 1890, when Ames made known that he had served long enough as president and when his mantle was about to fall upon the shoulders of Taussig, the decision was made by the directors — reluctantly — to let Waterman go ahead with his new promotions in Boston and to replace him with a superintendent who would devote his whole time to the Society's affairs.

After leaving the Society, Waterman remained a few years in the bookselling and stationery business in Boston. Then he went to New York where he developed a fountain pen which he had invented. His brother, L. E. Waterman, had invented in 1884 and later perfected the high-quality fountain pen which we all know. Our Arthur A. Waterman had a pen of his own with its special advantages. A lawsuit ensued and Arthur A. Waterman sold out his business interests in New York. Thereupon, in 1906, he moved West, living first in Chicago and then in Minneapolis. In the latter city he established a firm for repairing fountain pens and carried on a successful business not only repairing pens but putting on the market a silver polish and toilet preparations of his own concoction. In his old age he returned East, where he died in 1939.

Waterman had gone to Harvard to learn from books but stayed on to learn from life. Throughout his long business career, he pursued learning and esteemed men and institutions of higher education. He had sold and published books. He made and repaired pens, but he never used a pen to record the facts of his interesting life.

CHAPTER II

PROBLEM OF CONTROLLING THE SUPER-INTENDENT, 1890–1899

§1. Prosperity of the Society. The old ship continued to operate; only the captain was new. This new captain or superintendent, Charles D. Lyford, was hand-picked by a committee of the directors who apparently had several candidates to choose from. The directors had certain qualities in mind and thought they could see them in Lyford. Prominent among these was ability to push sales and to keep accounts straight. About the background of Lyford I have learned nothing. Presumably he came from some other retail store in the Cambridge or at any rate the Boston area.

The first year (1890–91) of Lyford's management saw sales go up from over $66,000 in 1889–90 to over $70,000. During the last year of his office (1898–99) sales reached $170,000. From 762 in 1889–90 the number of members changed as follows:

1890–91 —	987	1895–96 —	2,253
1891–92 —	1,299	1896–97 —	2,380
1892–93 —	989	1897–98 —	2,308
1893–94 —	1,681	1898–99 —	2,304
1894–95 —	1,909		

The increase in membership during the first two years is notable. During the year 1892–93, however, the membership lost the gains of the preceding years. This decline was checked and reversed by reducing fees from $1.50 to $1.00 per annum, at which figure they have remained ever since.

Under Lyford, dividends from $2,045.60 in 1889–90 were increased rapidly, 1890–99, as follows:

1890–91 — $2,800	1895–96 — $6,000
1891–92 4,000	1896–97 — 5,000
1892–93 — 5,000	1897–98 — 5,000
1893–94 — 5,000	1898–99 — 6,000
1894–95 — 5,000	

With this record, the ticket-holders must have been well satisfied. The directors, however, had a second reason to be gratified with the financial results obtained. The addition of net profits from the business (after a deduction of dividends) to capital and surplus was to the directors an assurance of smooth sailing. The additions to capital and surplus (in 1889–90 — $1,363.73) were as follows:

1890–91 — 1,963.74	1895–96 — 3,071.56
1891–92 — 3,272.07	1896–97 — 1,759.60
1892–93 — 2,543.81	1897–98 — 2,000.03
1893–94 — 2,328.95	1898–99 — 1,510.30
1894–95 — 2,761.07	

We can see in these figures an effort to follow the rule of 1888, namely, that the amount added to capital and surplus should be half the amount allotted to dividends. Even President Taussig, however, failed to follow this rule in his last year of office (1896–97), and President Wambaugh was a long way under the mark. Possibly the policy-formulators of the Society were beginning to feel that the capital and surplus (over $20,000) were adequate for current and future needs.

§2. Factors in prosperity. The course of business never runs smooth. This is as true of a co-operative society as of a non-co-operative firm. The fluctuations are the result of many variable factors, five of which may be considered. *First*, we should think of general business conditions. At once we discover that the continuously increasing volume of business done by the Society did not run parallel to the ups and downs of business prosperity in the country as a whole. Indeed, we are almost forced to conclude that in moderate depressions students bought more goods at the Co-operative because they had less money to spend and in years of moderate prosperity they bought more goods there because they had more money to spend. When general prosperity began to pick up during 1897–99, there was a slight drop in membership, though sales continued upward.

Second, the progressive increase in volume of sales was matched by a progressive increase in the number of students and instructors at Harvard. The following figures indicate the changes:

Year	Students	Instructors	Summer School
1890–91	2,271	242	279
1898–99	3,901	411	759

The clientèle of the Society was further increased in 1898 by the extension of the group to include alumni who, whether resident near or far, were finding the Society indispensable because only at the Society's store could they get the things they had come to want. Sales were made C.O.D.

The *third* factor was profit-sharing, which prevailed throughout the period. Indeed, the scheme seems to have been concocted before Lyford arrived and to have been introduced as a stimulus to sales. We recall that the first superintendent had once been rewarded by a share in the profits. Certainly, the plan could not have been designed to meet any high cost of living, because prices were at about their lowest in the period 1890–93–97. In truth, it was intended as part of a fresh management régime. A new sharing of profits and a new superintendent should bring prosperity. Such were probably the thoughts of President Taussig and the directors in 1890. But the profit-sharing was not confined to Lyford, the superintendent. There were probably three other employees besides Lyford in 1891–92, as we know there were in 1897–98, who shared in the profits. The working of the scheme is seen from the figures of 1897–98.

Employee	Rate	Base	Amount
Lyford	15%	$8,411.53	$1,261.73
Munro	4	"	336.46
Hall	4	"	336.46
Brooks	4	"	336.46
Total			$2,271.11

It is interesting to note that during the year 1897–98 the profits were divided as follows:

To the ticket-holders or members $5,000.00
To four employees 2,271.11

Of course, in addition to their profits (or commissions), the employees received regular salaries, Lyford beginning at $1,000 a year. Hall did so well in the book department that he also was given a bonus, one year of $90 and then $100. All this looks like fair treatment, and apparently the directors thought their policy was bringing the desired results. The system was swept away, however, on the departure of Lyford in 1899, after the Society had tried it for 10 years.

The *fourth* factor may have been the Society's own administration, particularly under the leadership of Taussig, who was president 1890–94 and 1895–97. There was a disposition on the part of the policy-formulators (officers and directors) to be effective, but leadership clearly lay with President Taussig. The president was young and ambitious. He had been made assistant professor of Political Economy in 1886 and full professor in 1892. Whether he was led to interest himself in the Society, first as director (since 1883) and then as officer, because of his early life in the co-operative West (St. Louis) or because his subject of political economy drew him toward business, is not clear. Although the son of a business man, Taussig never allowed the reality of economic life to encroach upon theory. This seems like a strange opinion in view of the fact that his *Tariff History* (1888), *Silver Situation* (1892), and *Wages and Capital* (1896), all reflect current interests, but they were public interests. What I mean is that Taussig was not for any long period occupied or concerned with business administration. It is reported that, when in 1908 President Eliot offered him the deanship of the Harvard School of Business Administration, he refused. In 1918 he remarked to the author that his position of chairman of the Tariff Commission was interesting but intellectually unsatisfactory. Although Taussig had many business men among his friends, still he had more real sympathetic interest in minority causes than in successful business. He was a liberal, almost a radical liberal (but not a social economist), and probably as such he found a challenge in the efforts of students to provide themselves with necessary supplies at reduced costs. We shall come back to Taussig and his work later in this chapter.

Whether Taussig was an economic theorist and not a business man is not the main point. The fact is that he was responsible for some good business practices. He and his directors (nominally) reviewed the accounts of the Society once a month. The board of directors was divided into groups, each of which was charged with special oversight of a certain department. Stimulus to increase the sales was provided by a profit-sharing scheme. And the surplus was increased to ample proportions, partly that the credit of the Society might be kept high and cash discounts obtained on purchases.

A *fifth* factor may have been the development of new lines of goods and new services. In this diversification of products there would be a widening of opportunities, of which more and more students would want to take advantage.

§3. Departments in the store — goods and services provided by the Society. There was a progressive increase in the number of commodities offered by the Society and some additions from time to time in the services performed for members.

By 1893 there were four outstanding departments recognized in the records — men's furnishing, book, stationery, and tailoring. Sometimes furniture (second-hand) and coal and wood were listed: in fact, they were hang-overs from the very first year of the Society. By 1895 a shoe-mending department had been added, and in 1896 the Medical Branch store seems to have made its appearance — the Society's first branch (lasting till 1903).

The men's furnishing department included fine clothing, athletic goods, and a complete laundry service — all these by 1893, and some a few years earlier. The tailoring department was located off the Harvard Yard — at 19 Brattle Street — and employed 5 hands. It was investigated in 1894 by a committee of the directors and given a satisfactory rating. Apparently, it took charge of the mending of students' clothes, which were put out to needy women in Cambridge working at so much per hour. Thus, apparently the Society was operating a sweatshop industry, which did not sweat — not if the rate per hour was fair or liberal.

The enumeration of departments gives us little notion of the commodities carried by the store. For instance, in 1893 the stationery department was credited with the following articles besides stationery — mathematical instruments, articles used in fine arts courses, fine cutlery, druggists' sundries (such as toilet articles and sponges), and inks and mucilage.

The existence of the departments was recognized in the accounting statistics compiled, particularly for stocks on hand and gross profits. Some of the statistics of stocks on hand are of interest.

STOCK BY DEPARTMENTS, 1894–98

Department	1894–95	1895–96	1896–97	1897–98
Men's Furnishing	$5,806.62	$5,000.00(!)	$3,941.88	$5,768.13
Book	4,017.33	5,654.49	6,173.43	5,996.34
Stationery	5,021.99	5,731.48	5,241.71	5,850.83
Tailoring	734.00	992.98	1,284.64	1,465.30
Shoe-mending	......	71.70	20.50	72.77
Medical Branch	......	3,623.49	7,730.86	8,314.87
Total	15,579.99(sic)	21,074.15(sic)	24,393.02	27,468.24

Beginning in 1890, the president was authorized to divide the board of directors into committees, each of which would be specially charged with the oversight of a department. Of course,

DANE HALL ABOUT 1890, THE SOCIETY'S THIRD HOME, 1883–1903

each department had a head and assistants. But departmentalization did not extend to the independent purchase of goods, as it does today (except for the adding of new lines of commodities). Thus, the store was somewhere between a general students' store and a students' department store in the period 1890–99.

§4. Difficulties of controlling management. Someone writing in a College paper during the earlier period had spoken of the Co-operative as "practical political economy." In every sense, that is just what business is not. The classical economics of Taussig gave scant recognition to business administration. And so the professor of Political Economy, the professor of Sociology, and the professor of Law had little or no theoretical background for his job as president during this period. Each had common sense, or perhaps uncommon sense, and wrestled with the problems accordingly.

One of the chief problems of business is control of administration by the stockholders and, beyond this, control of management by the chief executives. Of control of administration by the Society's members, there is little evidence. The Harvard student body has never been interested in controlling the Co-operative, at least not for any extended period. The chief executives (officers and other directors), however, have been much concerned with the need for control of those engaged in actual management — the superintendent and his assistants. During the period 1890–99 there was keen consciousness of the problem.

The office of treasurer was abolished in 1890 and was not re-established until 1902. Apparently, the incumbents of that office — students and instructors — had found little time, and were quite untrained, for the work involved. Henceforth, the duties of the treasurer were to be performed partly by the secretary and partly by the directors, each examining the accounts as they were (theoretically) passed around every month. How perfunctory such examination was may be easily imagined. Few undergraduates or instructors are keyed to this kind of routine; and, without the guidance of a specialist, such as a well-qualified treasurer, they would be quite uncritical. There was no executive committee to act for the board of directors. The substitute was the division of the board into separate committees, each to have supervision over a special department. This reminds us of the Harvard visiting committees and suggests the ease with which nothing would eventuate.

The frequent lack of a quorum must have bothered both President Taussig and President Wambaugh (1897–99). There was nothing to do except to pass a rule (1894) that, if a member of the board of directors was absent for two meetings without being excused, he should be considered as having resigned. All the officers and other directors were busy men and no fees were available to stimulate their memories to guide their bodies to the board meetings.

The volume of sales, number of departments, size of sales force, and extent of the store required some effective mechanical control. When Lyford came in 1890, it was hoped that he would facilitate this control by developing and perfecting a system of accounting. Probably he did much along this line but not enough. The advance of accounting in America and elsewhere has been slow and painful. The aims and methods have had to grow. The stockholders, the policy-formulators, and the management have all participated. The Harvard Co-operative has been typical in its struggle for better methods and clearer aims.

§5. Financial and cost accounting. The subject of accounting, like the subject of banking, is one that the citizen and general student turn from as from death and taxes. In truth, however, accounting is still just a system of common-sense reckoning of positions. It is by no means confined to business. Presbyterians and Jews are said by Werner Sombart to keep constant account with the deity so that there may always be a balance in their own favor.

In the old days, even till the end of the last century, accounts were kept in books, commonly in big books. In the Middle Ages these were bound in pigskin or vellum and often were held together by stout leather thongs. In the modern period the account books have been large, stiff-backed volumes, from one to five inches thick, containing paper pages specially ruled for the purpose to be served. In 1899 an outside auditor listed the Co-operative's five sets of account books as follows: Sales, Cash, Invoice, Journal, and Ledger. He might have added Wage Book, and he did recommend a Stock Record which would constitute a check to the movement of goods and make clear the condition of stock "at any time." All these books have now disappeared: perhaps some of them were destroyed when the Society moved across the Square from Dane Hall to Lyceum Hall in 1904, or when it tore down the old Lyceum building and erected the present store in 1924–25.

From the first, the Co-operative has prepared and preserved two sets of summary financial accounts. One of these is the operation statement which is designed to show profit or loss for a definite period. Under the first superintendent the annual statement of profit and loss was regularly prepared and also sometimes a semi-annual statement. The directors had wanted the superintendent to present a monthly statement, but he thought that the annual and semi-annual statements were all he could manage. Under the second superintendent weekly statements of business being done were apparently attempted but were soon abandoned (1895) in favor of monthly statements, and even these did not always appear. On one occasion, a special sample weekly statement, comparing current operations with those of the preceding year, was prepared and published. Some of the annual reports are the very essence of brevity and not at all explicit. Take, for instance, the following "Report" for 1895–96.

Stock	M.F.	5000.
	B.D.	5654.49
	S.D.	5731.48
	T.D.	992.98
	S.M.D.	71.70
	Med.	3623.49
	Total	21074.15

Expense 9225.32
Sales 150572.26
Members .... 2252.
Dividend .... 6000.
Profit 14370.79

As this statement stands, we cannot be certain that the profit-sharing commissions were included as expense or whether the profit item was the net profit from sales or from total operation.

The balance sheet is a statement of assets and liabilities, one side balancing the other. The fundamental purpose is to show the state of solvency. The early balance sheets of the Society, anxiously scanned in the difficult year 1884–85, were little more than balances of current assets and current liabilities, with the excess of assets over debts due put down as present worth, net present worth, or the "Society." These three last-named terms connoted capital. Then came the additional item of surplus or, as it was called, profit and loss. (The term "undivided profits" did not occur in early days.) We may clearly speak of capital and surplus before the incorporation of 1903 as after that event. During this period, 1890–99, the growing "capital and surplus" was still invested in current assets, the one exception being fixtures, which were of moderate value. Gradually, as the "capital" item was built up, it assumed more importance and came to be divided into capital and surplus. Much later, when real estate was acquired, a great deal of the capital and surplus represented this one item. Generally speaking, at that later period, the item of non-current assets and liabilities was substantial. On the whole, the evolution of the Society's balance sheet is a typical ontogenetic exhibit.

Cost accounting came into American business, generally speaking, during the late nineteenth century. The Co-operative Society does not seem to have lagged behind general business in the introduction of the concept and in making an effort to follow it up in practice, though relatively little progress was made during our present period of the management of Lyford. In 1893 Taussig stated that, in co-operative societies, the danger point was being reached when the cost of sales became 10 per cent of the volume of sales. Apparently with this in mind, figures of costs were compiled, recorded, printed, and commented upon. The following figures set forth the general expense ratio:

1891 — .0985(?) %   1893 — .0992%
1892 — .0995   1894 — .1058

Thus we see that the supposed danger point was never far away and was passed in 1894. At a later date (1901) a committee on expenses disclosed that these ratios were in fact false. The report reads in part as follows:

The strikingly 'low' expense percentage in our business, a fertile source of self-congratulation hitherto, has been especially a feature to which our presidents, at past annual meetings, have pointed with excusable pride. The committee can only regret that this feature did not have a better foundation in fact; and that the Board should have been misled into congratulating itself over a % expense rate, when the true rate was nearly one-half larger. ·

The committee added that "by the additional book-keeping jugglery we would have been able to run our business without any expense at all."

In order to make cost accounting more effective, costs should have been broken down at least to the department level. I have seen no indication that this was done, and, indeed, in 1899 an inquiry among the heads of departments elicited the statement that there was no departmental allowance for depreciation. This being the case, there could be no acceptable cost accounting for departments.

There was a dawning consciousness of the need for allowance for depreciation. In 1891–92 and following, we find 10 per cent deducted from net profits on sales (after expenses, but not commissions, had been subtracted). This was a depreciation allowance for merchandise. It was called a sinking fund. The depreciation of 10 per cent on fixtures had been deducted before the recording of the fixtures item. Hence, no matter how inadequate the application, the concept and practice of allowing for depreciation were in effect by 1891–92.

Clearly, the officers and directors of the Society were accounting-conscious during the period under review. This attitude was probably accentuated by developments in Massachusetts legislation. In 1896, it was provided that corporations with a capital of $100,000 or more had to have their accounts examined and certified by an auditor. Although this law did not apply to the Co-operative Society, which at the time was not a corporation and did not have a capital of the specified amount, still the discussion of the new requirement probably had influence on at least some of the officers and directors.

As early as 1891 the directors had authorized President Taussig to have an expert examine the books of the Society. Apparently nothing was actually done at the time. In 1896, at the suggestion of President Taussig, the board of directors authorized the president to arrange to have the company that bonded the superintendent also "inspect the books of the Society." In 1898 action was definitely taken in the direction of an outside audit. In 1899 a careful and extended investigation was made and this was followed by a report.

The auditor's report of 1899 showed that one account disagreed with another, notably the sales as found in the Sales Books and in the Ledgers. Many receipted bills were hard to find or missing. There was no Stock Record at all. And, on the whole, by implication, there was too little check on possible manipulation.

Now, it is instructive to consider the impact of all this on the president of the Society, Professor Taussig. His preoccupation with the affairs of the Society could not make him a business economist, for he was already too deeply concerned with classical or neo-classical economics. In other words, his life's interest had been fixed. But the problem of accounting came home to Taussig in a way not generally known and with results not commonly appreciated even by those close to the situation.

Taussig had doubtless observed his own lack of accounting expertness and had been impressed with the shortcomings of

PROFESSOR FRANK W. TAUSSIG IN 1901, PRESIDENT 1890–94, 1895–96

the treasurers of the period 1883–90. His fellow-officers and the other directors under his two presidencies may well have displayed the same lack of accounting skill. Probably he asked himself the question why it should happen that instructors and students interested in such a business as the Co-operative should be so much at sea in the realm of accounting.

This reflection probably led to an effort to remedy the situation by introducing a course of accounting into the curriculum of Harvard College. To this end, Taussig approached Mr. William Morse Cole (Harvard A.B., 1890). Mr. Cole had been instructor in political economy, working with Taussig, 1890–93. Then, while Mr. Cole was a teacher of English in high schools, first in Fall River and then in Worcester, during the period 1898–1908, Taussig asked him to give a course in accounting at Harvard. Taussig thought that Mr. Cole's training in economics together with considerable experience in accounting and a business college education equipped him for the work.

Mr. Cole became instructor in the Principles of Accounting at Harvard in September, 1900. When asked to undertake the work, he looked into the courses being given at the Wharton School of Finance and Commerce but found that they were mere book-keeping. Hence he was forced to fall back upon his own training and experience. His course was taken by about 35 men the first year, but carried no credit. Then, a *Crimson* canvass discovered that this course was ranked by the students as fourth in popularity among college courses. Credit was soon allowed for the work.

When Taussig raised the question of Mr. Cole's giving a course in accounting, he indicated that he had been thinking also about a school of business. This was during the academic year 1899–1900. Taussig concluded, however, that a school of business would be an uncertain venture and that beginning instruction in accounting was the immediately practical move to make.

Taussig did not drop the idea of a school of business, however, and even went so far as to ask Mr. Cole to draw up a scheme for a general business course to be given in the College.

Mr. Cole did this but does not now look upon his educational plan with any degree of satisfaction, for he did not envisage the subsequent developments that have taken place at Harvard. How near in point of time to the actual foundation of the Graduate School of Business Administration in 1908 was this final discussion between Taussig and Cole, I have not determined. When the School was actually established, it was the work of President Eliot and Professors Archibald C. Coolidge and Edwin F. Gay. Coolidge had been urging a school for training consuls, but Eliot found that impractical and saw in Professor Gay a promising leader with fertile imagination for the execution of Taussig's general idea.

Now, what I am getting at is the likelihood that Taussig's experience in the Harvard Co-operative Society did two things for education. First, it led to the earliest real course in accounting principles (as distinct from book-keeping practice) in the United States. (I assume that Professor H. R. Hatfield's work did not precede Professor Cole's.) Second, it led to a discussion of business training in general, out of which grew the Harvard School of Business. It is interesting to recall that Taussig always had a friendly interest in the School of Business, though for a period he was somewhat motivated by the idea that such a School would employ the young Ph.D.'s in economics which he as head of the department of Economics was having increasing difficulty in placing in teaching jobs.

§6. The second superintendent is dropped, 1899. Throughout the period of Lyford's tenure of office, the chief executives and other directors were fearful of ineffective accounting. By December, 1898, there were clear-cut suspicions that something was wrong, especially in the men's furnishing department. The superintendent was disinclined to give the names of the firms from which he was buying goods for this department. Then, the auditor's report, in March, 1899, showed serious general shortages as follows:

1896–97 — $2,829.58
1897–98 — 4,164.17

In the book department the average shortage was almost $1,000 a year for 4 years. Indeed, there was a "serious leakage in all three departments [men's furnishings, books, stationery] of the Cambridge store." The resignation of Lyford, the directors voted, should be accepted, but there was uncertainty as to when it should take effect. Then, on April 12, 1899, came a routine vote of the board of directors wherein confidence in the superintendent's integrity and appreciation of his services were expressed. Lyford resigned as of May 1.

What really went on in the meeting of the board of directors is not clear from the minutes. Only one member, the secretary-treasurer, was dead against Lyford. At one point, this secretary-treasurer's integrity was questioned by someone at a board meeting, on the ground that he might personally use the information he was securing in his investigation of the Society's affairs. He was exonerated, however, by a vote of confidence. It would appear, as it was later stated by Professor Albert Bushnell Hart, that it was a student who insisted on an outside audit. This student was the secretary-treasurer, W. E. Weaver, of the Law School. The faculty members were complacent, deceived, or ignorant of accounting realities. It was a Law School Professor (Ames) who had saved the Society in 1885. Now it is a Law School student who clears the atmosphere of muddle and incompetence and leads to the dismissal of the superintendent. What came out in the audit is the proof that the accounting of Lyford had proved ineffective: it was not up to the standards of the public accountant employed to investigate the system of accounts. We remember that the books of the first superintendent had been in an even worse condition.

It seems unfair to Lyford to record the vote of confidence and still not explain the well-established shortages in his accounts. At this stage, we can only surmise what really happened in the keeping of accounts. One source of error may have been the payment of bills which were not filed or recorded. Another source of shortage may have been other persons' theft from within or without, which could not be checked because of the lack of a Stock Record. In truth, we are left with uncertainty as to which was the more likely explanation of shortage, a bad system of accounting or an inadequate carrying out of the system established. Probably both theory and practice were at fault.

For Lyford there had been little enthusiasm. Little loyalty was displayed, partly perhaps because he was not a Harvard graduate! The personality of Lyford does not stand out in any respect. True, he made an effort to succeed and he had given his full time to the job of management. Whence he came and whither he went is unknown to me.

Getting a good manager is difficult in any business. Getting one for a co-operative society is even harder, that is, a manager who is at once able and honest. Controlling a manager in a co-operative society presents special difficulties because the policy-formulators — the officers at the top — are generally not familiar with the problems of management. In this case, they were doing their best, and the advice of the auditor showed them that they could never succeed while they employed Lyford. And so, a second well-meaning manager went on to other fields of operation — probably in Boston.

If we could have the story from Lyford, it would probably include three points. First, he stood on his record of ever-increasing sales rather than of expert accounting. Second, it was the system of accounting previously adopted and not he who was at fault. Had there been a controller in charge of accounts, he (Lyford) would have been held blameless. Third, the responsibility must be shared by untrained professors and students, making up the administration, who meant well but were too often shooting in the dark.

The period of Lyford's management coincided with the experiment in profit-sharing. Why profit-sharing went out with Lyford is not clear. The opinion had been expressed that Lyford had been too well paid. Some may have thought that, to the employees concerned, profit-sharing was a temptation that might lead to an unauthorized sharing called peculation. But there may have been no other thought than that, in a co-operative store, there was really no place for profit-sharing which looked to the pushing of sales, for this plan would be unfortunate in leading to frequent discontent with over-purchases and to the too frequent return of merchandise bought.

CHAPTER III

LAYING NEW FOUNDATIONS, 1899–1906

§1. The Medical Branch manager in charge, 1899–1903. F. H. Thomas had been manager of the Medical Branch in Boston since at least 1896–97, when he received $1,000 a year. That he was regarded as successful is indicated by the fact that his salary was next year raised to $1,200 and in addition he was given 20 per cent of the net profits. And so, in 1899 when Lyford left, Thomas, as a successful branch manager, was next in line. He seemed anxious to become superintendent of the Main Store, perhaps partly because his salary would be raised — actually it was raised to $3,000, but without any share in profits.

The officers and directors had no intention of lying down on their jobs just because they had a superintendent of proved merit. In fact, they were very active both in considering policies and in descending to petty managerial details. They agreed to buy a mirror, made a big point of adjusting wages even of the minor clerks, and appropriated various sums for advertising (particularly in the *Crimson*). Clearly, they had become expense-conscious. This was definitely registered by the appointment of a committee on expenses which turned in a strongly worded report on May 14, 1901. We shall come back to this report again, but at least we should note now the fact that the officers and other directors were serious, even wrought up, about their ineffective control of management.

During the period of Thomas' tenure of office we observe a number of minor though significant happenings. In 1901, the store was kept open till July 31, apparently to profit by the summer-school session. The directors were voted a fee of $2.00 for each meeting of the board attended. The president was to receive $800 a year and the secretary $10 for each meeting attended, provided that he made a record of the proceedings. Consideration was given to the addition of an alumni director. The purchase of a horse and wagon was authorized in 1901. A more liberal policy in buying textbooks was decided upon, as it had often been before. In 1902 the "optical branch" was to be enlarged and the "fancy groceries" abandoned.

But the old issue of control of the superintendent was still uppermost. Without this, the officers and directors seemed like an unanchored balloon. Without a knowledge of business and fully occupied with more favored pursuits, they felt that they had to have some mechanical device for controlling operations. Accounting was the only instrument. Big business was making similar discoveries at the same time.

Depreciation in departments and in the business as a whole was provided for throughout the period. A Stock Record was in use. An experiment was made in three departments for a two-fold reckoning of prices in stock-taking, namely, by wholesale and retail prices. When an assistant bookkeeper was to be employed, a graduate of a business college was to be preferred.

Thomas had not been in office for two years before a cleavage of feeling began. The same secretary-treasurer (W. E. Weaver, Law School student) who had sunk his teeth deep into the haunches of Lyford soon got scent of Thomas. In the report of the committee on expenses, referred to above, Weaver and a fellow committee-man pointed out that Thomas had unfortunately adopted the same system of reckoning expenses as had been followed by Lyford. This system took into account only the expenses of three out of the seven departments. Accordingly, the board of directors had been badly in error when in the previous fall they had published their estimate of annual expenses as under $18,500, while in fact the expenses soon proved to be over $27,000. In addition, a serious discrepancy in the working of the stock-checking system occurred in 1902. Next year there was considerable shrinkage in stock and a feeling that there had been poor styling in the men's furnishing department. In spite of the shortcomings of the superintendent, his books were finally found by an auditor to be "in fairly good condition."

The solution of the difficulty came through Thomas' offer to buy out the Medical Branch and resign the superintendency. Thomas probably felt that he knew the Medical Branch work and could succeed in the Boston store. The officers and other directors liked the idea, apparently because it got rid of the Branch and the superintendent at one time.

The Medical Branch was sold to Thomas for $2,500 cash, plus the value of the inventory. Thus, the goodwill was reckoned at $2,500. Thomas had to agree to sell goods to officers and students of the Medical School at a discount of 10 per cent as long as he occupied the store. Only by threat of a lawsuit could the F. H. Thomas Company be made to remove the Society's sign from its store. Nothing had been said about this in the contract. Indeed, there are probably several university stores in America where a sign bearing the words "Co-operative Society" is falsely displayed.

Just why the Society should have been willing to sell the Medical Branch, can be only surmised. The profit had not been very great. Indeed, three departments of the Main Store were more profitable. Probably the chief issue was the difficulty of management. One manager of the Branch had to be replaced even while Thomas was superintendent in the Cambridge Store. If the officers and other directors found difficulty in controlling a store located at Harvard Square, how much more helpless must they have felt when confronted with the problem of the store on Boylston Street. Probably a store in Boston was harder to manage not only because it was far afield but also because Boston bookstores, as I have been informed, had commonly given a discount of 10 per cent to customers. It may have been that, then as now, competing firms (today even from New York) sent their agents to the Medical School to sell off students' supplies at a little more than the retailer's cost at the beginning of the terms. At any rate, since 1903, when the Medical Branch was sold, it has ceased to be co-operative. Later, branches of the Society were to be established and run successfully but they were nearer at hand and not subject to such competition.

§2. The need for reorganization, 1892–1902. As early as 1892, the board of directors authorized President Taussig and the secretary (a senior) "to take steps leading to incorporation of the Society." No action seems to have followed this vote. In 1901, at a general meeting of the Society, Professor Jens I. Westengard, of the Law School, moved that the board of directors be authorized to prepare plans (a) for the reorganization and incorporation of the Society and (b) for handing over the corporation to "a reasonably stable body of stockholders [trustees]." Early in 1902, M. A. Sullivan, a director and Law School student, called for action under the earlier vote. A revolutionary movement was on foot. The first phase was under the leadership of Professor Westengard and failed; the second was under the leadership of Professor Ames, also of the Law School, and succeeded. We shall examine each of the situations, but first let us look at the need for change — the background of the revolution. Parenthetically, I find it interesting to recall the fact that an old-timer, long prominent in the Society, recalled the revolution but could not remember what was revolutionized.

For some time, there had been misgivings, particularly among the faculty officials of the Society, that the unincorporated group was in an exposed position. The members were individually liable for all the debts of the Society. Moreover, if any move should be made to purchase a building, there would be difficulty not only in the matter of individual liability but in the matter of the special liability of the officers. Already, leases had had to be signed by officers assuming individual responsibility. The Society was growing too big, so it was thought, for this kind of situation.

The other part of the change had to do with control of the corporation which was to be set up. The members had not functioned. It was said that never had over 50 members attended a general meeting. Often only about 5 members appeared, and they voted for the roster of officials and other directors proposed by the nominating committee of the old board of directors. One commentator said that the only persons that you could be sure would attend the annual meeting were a reporter from the *Crimson* and a freshman who wanted to take everything in. Actually, in this great emergency, when the new constitution was voted on, only about one-fifth of the members participated by casting their ballots. It is clear to me that student co-operation in administration had never taken hold in the Harvard Co-operative. And so the proposal was, in part, to find an effective substitute — permanent stockholders who would act as trustees for the members or ticket-holders. This would not interfere with sharing in profits on purchases.

It is rather interesting to note that certain members of the Society feared that some day a handful — maybe only thirty — of the members might put through an unannounced revolution. Better by far, they thought, to have a constitutional revolution than a *coup* that would change everything — perhaps even declare that all net profits should be paid out as dividends!

The members of the Society seem to have divided into four groups according to the positions they took. One group, led by the officers and other directors, wanted both a corporation and a trusteeship. A second, headed by Professor Albert Bushnell Hart, did not think a corporation really necessary and strongly objected to any trusteeship. Professor Hart had stated in a *Crimson* article that he had had experience as a director of the Society, but he did not say that he rarely was present at meetings. Nothing is clearer than that he had an ingrained opposition to management by cliques and a strong feeling for democracy, as witness his championship of the Bull Moose Campaign of 1912. A third position was sponsored by M. A. Sullivan, already mentioned, who saw the need for a corporation but thought that the members should continue to have the power to vote for officers and other directors. True, not many would turn out on ordinary occasions but, when there was something really important, enough would appear to do the job that was required. The fourth group was the largest, being made up of about four-fifths of the members of the Society. This group was indifferent to all constitutional and legal matters. It was much interested in the chance to buy a wide variety of acceptable goods and mildly interested in the dividends paid. It exemplified the economic man.

In passing, I cannot help reflecting that the student participation, which the chief executives of the Society were so anxious to render as innocuous as it had proved to be sporadic, had on rare occasion really shown capacity for leadership. I recall Kip, the intellectual father; Bolles, the able formulator of the first constitution and also the first president; Weaver, the law student, who as secretary-treasurer insisted on reform and efficiency in accounting; and Sullivan, the only director who stood out, at least in any active way, against submerging the democratic privilege of voting. We recall that a hundred years earlier in Boston there had been a lawyer, James Sullivan, who was also a great democrat.

An outstanding issue was being drawn. Should the original democratic way of life prevail or a new aristocratic oligarchy be adopted? The democratic way was lazy and normally inoperative, wasteful and expensive, unstable and uneven. It was the hard way that required education and leadership. The aristocratic way was to give power to the best qualified — the teachers and especially the administrative group of teachers — so that dividends would be forthcoming, a capital built up, and slow, conservative growth insured. The Harvard faculty and student body were called upon to make the decision. Harvard stood for education and was challenged in 1902 to decide whether education would work in a co-operative society. Other colleges decided on the democratic way of government but lost the co-operative way of doing business, or limped along with starved co-operative societies. Too often, they kept the memory but lost the thing. American business generally was becoming firmly entrenched in financial capitalism or control by Wall Street. Mergers and trusts were in the air and were becoming realities — the strong business units of today. Professors and students at Harvard were asked to make their choice.

The issue was clear enough as between the two extremes. Perhaps neither extreme would prove to be necessary. A compromise might be devised. Knowing the spirit of Harvard, I should think that the emphasis would be put upon reality but that provision would be made for the ideal.

§3. Incorporation and trusteeship, 1902–1903. The move to reorganize the Society came apparently from the professors, and leadership was assumed by the board of directors dominated by the professors. This was not a popular revolution nor was it primarily of the nature of a palace revolution, though before the matter was ended there was something like this in sight. Let it not be thought that I am making too much of the whole affair: this has been the sole instance in its sixty years' existence of popular interest in the Society's government.

On May 29, 1902, the board of directors proposed incorporation and by-laws to govern the new corporation. Foremost among these were three new arrangements that were far-reaching. First, the stock of the Society should be "vested in a reasonably stable body of stockholders." Second, the ticket-holders (members) of the future were expressly excluded from the administration of the Society. Third, the old members and new ticket-holders were to have no financial responsibility in the Society's affairs, though they were to continue to receive on their purchases such dividends as might be declared by the board of directors.

Now, it is to be noted that the stockholders were all to be members of the faculties of Harvard University, and as trustees, to represent the membership of the Society. It was to be expected that there were enough students at Harvard of Revolutionary and Irish descent to object to this. When the vote of June 6, 1902, was announced, the spirit of 1776 was shown to have survived by eight votes. The new constitution was lost, but not irretrievably. The spirit of the eight might be crushed as the power of Spain had just been crushed. The *Crimson* had done its best in helping free and outspoken discussion; it was to continue to assist in further argumentation.

We may infer that the general plan of incorporation and trusteeship in this era of merger prosperity in America was not itself unpopular at Harvard. Only special points and particular persons were objectionable. Reading the College papers of the time, I conclude that the personnel of the five stockholders was not attractive: the individuals were just professors and without distinction, except that two were downright unpopular. The board of directors that sponsored the reorganization contained two or more members whom the students did not like. In addition, the power given to the stockholders appeared to be excessive, and no alternative method was left for choosing officers and other directors. Anglo-Saxon constitutionalism could not tolerate so radical a break. Some concessions must be made to the unworkable ideals of the past.

Wise men, good friends of the Society, saw that only a little patching was really required. A new committee was formed, headed by the savior of 1885, Professor (and then Dean) James B. Ames, of the Law School. This committee, aided by Professor Bruce Wyman, also of the Law School, made proposals that corrected the weakness in the plan of the first committee.

The second plan named, as the initial stockholders, five of the strongest men connected with Harvard at the time, including Major Henry L. Higginson who had donated the Harvard Union. Moreover, none of the current officers or directors were included among the stockholders. Accordingly, there would be less chance for collusion between the stockholding trustees and the board of directors. Even more important was the provision for an alternative mode of election of officers and directors apart from any action of, and even in competition with, the stockholders. It was proposed that 25 participating members might nominate one or all of the officers and other directors; and, if there should be 100 members at the annual meeting who actually participated in the voting, then the nominees could be voted on. If any of these nominees received a majority of the votes (that is, 51 or more), they would be elected and would supplant the candidates supported by the stockholders.

Furthermore, the second plan stated that none of the stockholders might be officers or directors. This might be thought to resemble that vicious system of excluding owners from boards of directors, which exists in so many business firms today. In reality, however, the stockholders were mere trustees who held the stock in order to make wise choices of officers and other directors. They could never profit by their position, unless they should elect themselves as officers (the president and secretary received monetary rewards); and now even this loophole was closed. In addition, the powers and duties of the stockholders were subject to change by mutual consent of the stockholders and a majority of the participating members, if at least 25 per cent of the participating members should vote. And, finally, the Society was followed up even to death: it might be dissolved not only by the stockholders but by a majority vote of the participating members.

The result was that more members came out to vote on the second reorganization than on the first. On the first occasion 474 voted, on the second 571. What was more important, the vote was reversed: the majority of 8 against was turned into a majority of 363 in favor. And then, when the first annual meeting occurred (December 17, 1902), there was a contest! The stockholders were challenged. Although their candidates for treasurer and 7 directorates were accepted, their candidates for president, secretary, and one directorate were opposed. The total votes cast were 320. The opposition elected their candidate for president and for the one remaining directorate. Charles H. Ayres ('98), who had been in the Graduate School for three years, was chosen president. He was to be elected for three years in succession.

The 5 stockholders and 11 newly elected officers and directors thereupon petitioned the State for incorporation and received it on January 28, 1903. And so, the group, originally made up of free oppressed students, who in 1882 had gone out as petty capitalists to do battle with the other petty capitalists (retailers at Harvard Square), was becoming a "soulless corporation" in the régime of industrial capitalism. The gentlemen, learned in the law, had put their knowledge to good use. They had established an instrument of business in which one body checks another and in which there is a residual ownership but no man can find the owners. No radical minority — as these go at Harvard — is big enough to disturb the new equilibrium. Evolution is provided for; revolution is shut out. In the long service of the Law School to the Co-operative Society, a climax had been reached.

The judgment of Mr. Arthur A. Ballantine, who was long a member of the board of directors of the Society and who later became a national figure in law in New York and in governmental administration in Washington, is that "the application of that plan removed all complaints about the board. In fact, there has never been a call for an election. I believe that that idea could be most fruitfully applied in the field of industrial corporations."

§4. A new superintendent and a new building, 1903–1906. The year 1903 was a high point in the history of the Harvard Co-operative Society. It brought a new constitution, a new superintendent, and the ownership of a place of business. Having considered the constitution, we may now concentrate on the superintendent and the place of business. The period covered is from the incoming of the new superintendent, Laws, to the accession of Professor W. B. Munro as president of the Society.

Frederick A. Laws (1876–1912) was the fourth superintendent or manager of the Harvard Co-operative Society. He was born not far from Cambridge and was graduated from Harvard with his class in 1897. After leaving college, he entered the real-estate and insurance business, then the financial department of the American Express Company, and finally became superintendent of the Society, 1903–11. He left the Society for a job that some regarded as an advance, in the credit department of the Amoskeag Manufacturing Company in Boston (1911–12).

Laws was an amateur musician and belonged to several musical clubs. He was unmarried and lived for years at the old

Colonial Club in Cambridge, on the committees of which he put in a good deal of time. He was one of the founders of the Harvard Square Business Men's Association and was a member of other business associations. He took some courses in the Harvard School of Business and expressed great admiration for the leadership of Dean Gay. Certainly Dean Gay and many contemporary business men were emphasizing in theory what Laws was doing in practice — promoting business associations. "In all these circles," writes a correspondent, "his likeable qualities and capacity for staunch friendship were helpful factors in enhancing a feeling of friendliness toward the Society." Another, who also knew Laws intimately in the Society's operations, writes that he "was a likeable and reliable man, but he did not have the training and aptitude" necessary for a superintendent.

In 1904 proposals were made to the board of directors that the Society's store handle tobacco and establish a banking department. Nothing resulted from these suggestions. In 1905 the directors thought that the variety of ready-made clothing handled by the men's furnishing department should be increased. In 1906 a proposal was made to supply coal directly rather than through an outside firm. This was probably no more favorably considered than the suggestion that the Society should establish an express service.

In 1905 came the loss of the handling of law books. The Society informed the professors in the Law School that, since it was losing money on law books, it would have to raise the percentage of gross profit from 5 to 10 per cent. This was rejected by the professors of the Law School. Thereupon, the Society proposed a compromise, namely, that accounts for the books purchased should be settled in October rather than in December. Since this was likewise rejected, the law-book business was discontinued by the Society. We recall that two years earlier the medical book business was abandoned with the sale of the Medical Branch. Both legal and medical books are expensive and hard to make profitable. Thus, we see that, in the period 1903–05, profits had come to constitute a vital part of the Society's policy. Perhaps we had better express the policy in this way: no service at any considerable loss.

For years, members of the Co-operative have observed that a private bookseller has handled law books at Harvard Square, and they have wondered why this should be the case. If the story above had been narrated to these observers, the question would have arisen as to whether the Society had not acted in anger or in haste. I do not know the answer, but it is worth recalling that the president (Charles H. Ayres, Jr.) and two of the directors (Mr. A. A. Ballantine and Mr. Grenville Clark) were at the time students of law. On the surface, the issue seems to have been one of profits and that alone. Certainly, at a later date the Society sought to regain and finally did regain the business of providing law books on the basis of 10 per cent of the gross profit.

During the first years of the corporation's existence, with which we are dealing, 1903–06, the dominance of the policy-formulators (officers and other directors) was pronounced. Charles H. Ayres, after having served three years as director, was president for three years, 1902–05. He was instructor in physics at Harvard, 1901–05, and took a law degree in 1905. Mr. A. A. Ballantine served the Society with remarkable loyalty and obvious ability. He was director, 1901–05, and president, 1905–06; later (1908–18) he was to be secretary of the Society and to record the minutes with a new feeling for discriminating terminology. These 17 years of service are comparable with the 17 years of Professor Taussig. I think that we can say that both Ayres and Ballantine as presidents were familiar with the problems of the Society, kept right on their jobs, were anxious to make good, and soon became not unconscious of their power. Perhaps their feeling of responsibility was heightened by the difficulties of the times and the unfamiliarity of the new super-intendent with retailing.

During the management of Laws, sales went down in 1903–05 and then upward from 1905–06, continuing upward in fact, except for the war year 1917–18, to 1929–30. Membership declined till 1905–06 and then increased continuously till 1930–

31. The amount added to capital and surplus under Laws' whole period of management, 1903–11, was at the lowest point in the Society's history, though that did not mean very much in view of the investment in real estate.

The explanation of the poor showing in certain years of this period is, as usual, complicated. Sales went down partly because of the loss of the Medical Branch in 1903 and partly because of the decrease in the student body in the period 1903–08. The loss of sale of law books in 1905 would have been unfavorable to volume of sales but not to net profits. Perhaps the temporary general business set-back of 1903 had some effect on the Society's prosperity for two years. It is also possible that the new superintendent was not very helpful during these years.

During the years 1903–06, we find thefts, one forgery, and shortages in the men's furnishing and furniture departments. Dissatisfaction with the book department was expressed in 1904 and thefts of books in that department continued. It is interesting that the honesty of members did not increase with book knowledge. Or was the theft of books just an informal profit-sharing instituted by the non-members? In 1905 a catalogue of books was proposed as a check on theft and for the year 1905–06 this catalogue indicated that books having a sales value of $282.26 were missing.

Clearly, the officers and other directors were dissatisfied with Laws' management of the Society's affairs. In 1905 they ordered "that business may in the future be transacted more promptly." Complaint was made this same year that the superintendent had "no active interest in the shortages in the Book Department," and that he had not prepared the necessary figures for the board's consideration on a certain occasion. The superintendent's salary was left at $2,300, obviously as a censure for the "unbusiness-like way in which the affairs of the Society are being conducted." Whether it was the fault of the superintendent that less coal was being sold in 1906 and that it was poorer in quality and $1.50 a ton higher in price than elsewhere, is not known.

LYCEUM HALL IN 1908, THE SOCIETY'S FOURTH HOME, 1903–24

Right through the whole period 1903–06 goes the lack of confidence between the board of directors and the superintendent. The latter was given a lower salary than his predecessor had received and he was not invited to attend the board's meetings, as preceding superintendents had been on occasion. This fact indicates that the officers were partly at fault. Written reports are no substitute for oral discussion. The superintendent should have been dismissed or brought into the board of directors.

In any effort to understand the management difficulties of this period, it may be of significance to note that the new superintendent came in at almost the same time as the board of directors was charged with the task of leaving Dane Hall, located on the edge of the Yard, and of finding a new building elsewhere. After residence in Dane Hall from 1883 to 1903 the Society was informed that it must move. It chose to buy the Lyceum Hall in 1903 for $77,500, located across Harvard Square on the present site of the Main Store. Whereas since 1899 the Society had paid an annual rental of $1,000 to Harvard College, its cost of occupancy was henceforth to be over four times that amount (less and less reduced for a few years by a diminishing rental income).

The old Lyceum Hall had been used jointly by sundry firms — a gas company, an express company, a restaurant, and a billiard parlor. It was an outstanding building on an excellent site. The Lyceum property was purchased for cash raised by a mortgage loan from Harvard University to the amount of $50,000 at 4½ per cent, a series of loans on recurring notes at not over 5½ per cent, and the proceeds from the sale of the Medical Branch. The necessity of borrowing by notes created an almost constant item of business for several years.

It is not unlikely that the Society half welcomed the necessity of leaving the Yard. It had long been forced to locate its tailoring department elsewhere. It had been seriously burglarized on May 1, 1903 — to the extent of $1,080. But the deciding factor was that Harvard needed the space. There was apparently also the lurking anxiety that the Society's presence in a University building might impair the University's position as a tax-exempt institution. Clearly, the Society was emphasizing more and more the policy of profit-making for its services. Moreover, it had become a corporation and it smacked of private business. In addition, it was a trust and, as such, might in popular estimate be identified with the monopolistic trust which the Sherman Act was designed to destroy.

§5. The new foundation stones, 1899–1906. These were vitally important years for the Co-operative Society. We may well reflect on the meaning of what happened and what was in the process of unfolding.

Originally, the purpose had been to found a society which would reduce the price of goods and services at Harvard Square. This purpose was fulfilled. Then the emphasis turned to the making of profits for the members by serving them at a new price level, lower than the one that would have prevailed at the Square had the Society not been formed, and about the same as existed in Boston. These points have been demonstrated in preceding chapters. Now, in the period under discussion, the task became the creation of a solid basis for further growth.

The solid basis was the corporation controlled by stockholders who were co-optative. Henceforth, there were two entities living side by side and presided over by the same president. One was the new corporation. The other — bearing the same name — was the old unlimited partnership or association. This last-named body, formed in 1882, was in 1903 kept as a vestigial organ that in fact had long lost its early puny vitality as an economic democracy. In truth, a few men have from the first made the Society workable. This is just a bit of social reality that we may do well to remember.

One of the elements of growth in the Society that is hardest to trace is the weaving together out of experience all that had been thought of originally and all that had been learned subsequently. Co-operation was killed in actual administration, but it was kept alive (a) in the title, (b) in the sharing of the net profits, and (c) in by-laws which made possible a revival of

co-operative administration. The whole new arrangement was
entered into because the members wanted it thus.

One purpose of the reorganization of 1903 was to provide
continuity of administration. In reality, this was not to come
at once: we find it abundantly illustrated, however, in the next
two chapters in both the board of directors (officers and other
directors) and the (board of) stockholders.

During this period we find a larger measure of business-like
administration than ever before. The president was paid a
salary and the secretary and directors received fees. Beginning
in 1903, the treasurer, on the resurrection of his office, was paid
a salary. Moreover, the board of directors became more expense-conscious and assumed effective control of management.

The move of the Society from University property (Dane
Hall) paved the way for more unfettered action, such as the
extension to all-comers of the right to buy at the Society's
store. It facilitated also the later arrangement of bringing the
Massachusetts Institute of Technology into the membership
and administration of the Society. It is interesting to note that
the establishment of a branch store at, and in, the School of
Business in 1927 was by way of a retrogression from the policy
of not occupying Harvard buildings.

The success of the profit policy — one test of private business — was demonstrated when a total dividend payment of
over twice that of any previous year was declared in 1902–03
and when an addition was also made to capital and surplus.
Likewise, in this period, without ruining the working capital
position of the Society a piece of real estate was acquired that
was to prove of immense value. There are few college co-
operative societies in America that own their own places of
business.

So far, then, looking over the whole history of the Society up
to 1903, we find victorious in its evolution the following policies:

(a) Keeping down prices at Harvard Square to a level comparable
to those in Boston.

(b) Earning a net profit on sales of goods and services at the reduced
price level.

(c) Distributing part of the net profit as dividends to members up to 1902 and to ticket-holders from 1903 onwards.

(d) Building up a capital and surplus in order to secure a discount on purchases for cash, to avoid the embarrassment of an operating deficit, and to make possible the expansion of services.

(e) Solving the problems of management by employing an effective superintendent and a number of assistants, instituting the best methods of departmental operation, perfecting accounting as a source of financial information and as a device for controlling management, and employing an auditor, who had skill and impartiality, to discover facts and report them to the board of directors.

(f) Taking away from the old-time members the burden of administration and of unlimited liability, while leaving the right to share in profits.

(g) Providing for continuity of administration through a specially chosen group of men of administrative ability.

(h) Acquiring a building with a good location and of ample size for present operation and future expansion.

With such success, we might conclude that all was well with the Co-operative. In their reorganization of the Society in 1902–03, the lawyers had performed a masterful task in an effective manner. In their administration of the Society, 1903–06, however, they seemed to have accentuated an unfortunate cleavage in so far as they kept the superintendent — the management — at arm's length. They did not realize that in business both policy-formulation and control should be integrated with management and not superimposed upon it. In every institutional arrangement there seem to be something good and something bad, something perfect and something imperfect. In other words, in setting up and following out the new constitutional order, the lawyers split the administration even farther asunder — by separating the topmost policy-formulating and controlling body from the lower stratum of management. And so, there was further work to be done and more to write about in the next chapter.

CHAPTER IV

GROWTH AND STRONG ADMINISTRATION
1906–1919

THE PRESIDENT PLANS AND CONTROLS

§1. Professor Munro takes the president's chair. Ames, Taussig, and Munro were three professors who gave liberally of their time and attention to the Co-operative Society. William Bennett Munro (Queens LL.B., '98; Harvard Ph.D., 1900) became instructor in Government at Harvard in 1904, assistant professor in 1906, and professor of Municipal Government in 1912. He was an excellent teacher of undergraduates, clear in thought and expression, and orderly in the arrangement of his facts. Between 1909 and 1917 he wrote several books, principally on municipal government. During this period he was also very active in sundry local business, editorial, and constitutional affairs.

It is obvious that Professor Munro was busy, very busy, during the years of his presidency of the Co-operative Society, 1906–18. We may deduce that he spent more time in reading, writing, and attending meetings than in abstruse philosophical speculations concerning law and government. He was and is one of those rare persons who learn not only from books but also from life and in about equal proportions. While president of the Co-operative Society, he learned from observation that certain things should be done. He functioned like the mayor of a city who has to work closely with departments — the superintendent of the Co-operative Society, with a council — the board of directors, and with an electorate — the stockholders. He knew little about retailing at first hand, but he could make wise decisions concerning general policies and he could keep control over management. Like his two predecessors — also trained in the law, he was anxious to make good in his office; and with a wide fund of knowledge, excellent judgment, and a feeling for orderly procedure, he had an unusual opportunity to do so.

Professor Munro became the clear-cut embodiment of the "new order" in the affairs of the Co-operative Society — a new Munro Doctrine for the Society. He proudly and repeatedly announced that the Society was a business and not a charity. He was eager to discover and effect business-like methods. He insisted on efficiency of operation. He was a professor who was also an executive.

In a way, Professor Munro's supreme personal achievement was to have risen above the constitutional *status quo* of 1902–03. He was apparently not so impressed with the constitutional victory that he could see nothing further to do. It was his interest in, and insight into, administration, as distinct from constitution, that enabled him to accomplish what his predecessors in the president's chair, especially during the period 1903–06, had failed to see. Perhaps his familiarity as a student of government with the parliamentary system, as distinct from the congressional system, may have helped point the way to the conclusion that the Co-operative Society would never be on an administratively sound basis until the superintendent was either asked to attend the meetings of the board of directors or actually made a full-fledged member of the board. But Professor Munro assures me that an even greater influence was his familiarity with the English system of having a managing director. He wanted the superintendent to be given that title in addition to his regular one. Indeed, the two have been used ever since, formally or informally. Important as this matter was in itself, it was more significant in what it stood for, that is, the closely integrated functioning of the board of directors (officers and other directors) and the superintendent. Retailing is what retailing does. It cannot be learned from constitutions or from law. It is not capable of being reduced to rules. It is not today what it was yesterday. The superintendent on the job has the feeling of the living stream of effort required. He alone can

WILLIAM BENNETT MUNRO ABOUT 1930, PRESIDENT 1906–18, 1919–22

know the whole process of purchasing and selling, guiding his assistants, and controlling his stock. A board of directors can be intelligent only by using the superintendent's brains and experience. With this advantage, it can use the best abilities of its members to support or oppose, curtail or amplify.

From the administrative standpoint, the year 1908 was of great importance for the Harvard Co-operative Society. It saw the board of directors propose and the stockholders accept the superintendent as an *ex officio* member of the board of directors. It also saw the establishment of an executive committee of five members of the board who were to assist the president and were to make recommendations to the board. This committee was to be made up of the president, treasurer, secretary, and two others. In 1909 the superintendent was made *ex officio* a member of this committee. The third development during 1908 was the provision for an alumni director, who might be a business man. The first was Mr. Arthur S. Johnson ('85), of C. F. Hovey and Company, who was followed by Mr. Henry S. Thompson ('99), who has served the Society first as director (1910–21), then as vice-president (1921–22), and finally as president since 1922.

In a real sense, with the creation of the executive committee, the new framework of the Society's government was complete. The accompanying graph shows the parts of the framework and their inter-relations. The reader may want to return to this diagram frequently as he reads the pages that follow.

The inner meaning of the new administrative changes of 1908 is that the president of the Society at last had a small group, all specially chosen, who could give effective assistance (a) in preparing business for discussion by the board of directors, (b) in meeting weekly, if necessary, to look after pressing matters, and (c) in taking from the president's shoulders some of the jobs, such as negotiating a lease or making a special inquiry. The treasurer, since 1902, has been an official of Harvard (or, since 1940, of the Massachusetts Institute of Technology). The secretaries of the period 1902–18 were instructors at Harvard; since 1918 the secretary has been Mr.

Walter Humphreys, formerly of the faculty of the Massachusetts Institute, now secretary of its Corporation, who has specialized in executive secretarial work. The superintendents, of
course, have known the business itself. The alumni representa-

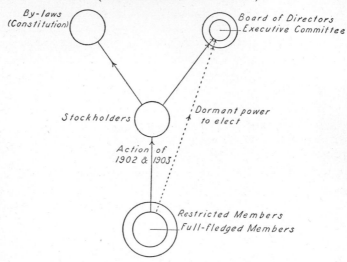

STRUCTURAL ANALYSIS OF THE CO-OPERATIVE
(Framework of Government)

tive has been a business man. Professor Munro leaned heavily
on Mr. A. A. Ballantine, who was secretary, 1908–18, and acted
as legal counsel without pay; on Dr. H. L. Blackwell ('99), who
was controller of the University, 1906–10, and a director of the
Society, 1903–24; and on Mr. Lincoln F. Schaub, who was assistant-dean of the School of Business, a director of the Society,
1910–18, vice-president, 1919–21, and president, 1918–19.
There is evidence of the influence of Professor Edwin F. Gay,
dean of the School of Business, not only on the stockholders
but (through President Munro) on the board of directors. In
short, it was President Munro who brought into the Society's
administration the specialized administrators of the University,
members of the School of Business, and actual business men.

In effect, this meant that business was taking the place of law in the affairs of the Society.

Perhaps at this point we may stop to note that there have been clear-cut steps in the history of the Co-operative's administration. At first, the students were alone in executive control. Then, the non-administrative faculty group took over the executive power. Now, in President Munro's day, domination passed, both in the board of directors and in the (board of) stockholders, to the administrative academic group, whether teachers or not. There was to be a fourth development, which we shall see in the next chapter, of bringing into greater control men actually in business — notably the manager himself and the president. When, on occasion, the undergraduates now wistfully wonder what they might do by way of participating in the affairs of the Society, they should reflect on the long distance that the administration has travelled since the days of Kip and Bolles.

In considering the administration of Professor Munro, we cannot fail to note the printed Annual Reports that he was responsible for. They show a grasp of current and long-time needs of the Society and display a power of presentation not exhibited before or since his day. Parenthetically, we may note that a reading of these Reports indicates that the early zeal of the years 1906–07 to 1911–12 was not maintained. Apparently, the directors thought that since the Reports were not taken or read by the members, they should be abbreviated. This was clearly a misguided policy. What was needed was a better system of distribution.

President Munro was interested in merchandising policies as well as administrative arrangements. He laid emphasis on the extension of sales, a rapid turnover of stock, an improved system of stock control, and a low ratio of cost of sales and general operation.

In the matter of pushing sales, President Munro was not content to enunciate a policy of aggression; he personally participated in the task of discovering new outlets and in arranging for the new business. Thus did the professor descend from policy-formulation to actual management, though not to routine management. When there was a decline in business in 1910, President Munro considered establishing a branch store at Radcliffe College and the re-purchase of the Medical Branch. It is interesting to note that efforts were made to get back the handling of Law School books. In 1911 he sponsored the move to have the Society act as purchasing agent for Harvard University in order to save money for the University and bring in a reasonable profit (in fact, little more than expenses) to the Society. The University baseball team and the College Library were similarly brought into the Society's net. He favored the placing of a representative of the tailoring department in Boston once a week to display goods, take orders, and make fittings, catering particularly to the needs of graduates of the University. When Thurston's stationery store got into difficulty, he favored buying it and running it as a branch on Massachusetts Avenue. He sponsored the adding of tobacco to the list of goods for sale. The vote was to the effect that "the experiment be made of selling tobacco in bulk at the store without conspicuous display, and with the understanding that cigars and cigarettes are not to be lighted in the store." President Munro favored the purchase of whole editions of authors' works (e.g., Taussig and Lowell) so as to reduce the cost to members. In 1913, however, he was opposed to the re-establishment of a line of groceries on the ground that this action would further antagonize the business men at Harvard Square and that groceries would not be demanded by the rank and file of the members. In 1916 he personally devised a mail-order business particularly for the sale of books and stationery to graduates and to schools and colleges in New England. Part of this, the sale of stationery, had to be abandoned in 1917 because of the difficulty of getting supplies. In general, the cost of this business (particularly the preparation of the catalogue of books) did not justify the effort. After considerable loss, the mail-order business in books was abandoned about 1925. Part of the plan was promising, namely, using the time of the staff in slack seasons and keeping in touch with graduates, even continuing their education by providing them with books. Unfortunately, the University had put on an endowment campaign which left the graduates too poor to buy books. But why emphasize this excuse? These same graduates had sold their books before leaving college: most of them had probably finished their education from books.

Although not personally interested in accounting as such, President Munro was keenly aware of the importance of an adequate system. He saw shortages and overages occurring in one department or another every year. The chief question was how much this year? This had been a thorn in the side of every superintendent and board of directors from the beginning. That overages occurred as well as shortages indicated that peculation was not the cause, or not an important factor. It was with great expectation that the new treasurer, John L. Taylor, arranged to have the auditors introduce a new accounting system designed for use in a department store, or, as President Munro put it, "an entirely new system of expense accounting." This went into effect on January 1, 1912. Henceforth departments were sharply divided and to each department was allotted its share of the cost of doing business. If fault should arise, then the blame could be allocated.

In 1912 an expense manager was provided for, and at once Mr. George E. Cole entered the store to embark upon a service which, with a minor break, in a sense still continues. His task was to keep expenses within the budget or supplementary budget. In addition, he was to develop a merchandise control which should be designed to keep the amount of stock on hand from becoming excessive. By 1914 it was considered that Mr. Cole had accomplished so much along these lines that he might safely be given a temporary leave of absence.

In 1914 J. A. Smith of the School of Business was asked to introduce a system of monthly statements concerning sales, expenses, and the stock of each department. Efforts to have adequate monthly statements for the use of the board of directors had been made from the early years of the first superintendent. Considering these statements still occupies a large part of the board's time and energy.

President Munro was intensely interested in the financial accounting and the story that it told from year to year. He was anxious to follow a conservative depreciation policy, so as to allow for the decline in value of merchandise and fixtures, doubtful accounts, and building. He was much concerned with the problem of accounts receivable, that is, the debts owed to the Society by customers. In 1911 he reported that $7,530.90 was over-due by three months. The board felt that, as far as possible, credit should be refused to those whose accounts were more than three months over-due. The president knew full well that credit was the rock on which many a co-operative ship had been wrecked. In 1913 came the ruling that no dividends would be paid on accounts that had run for three months or over. In 1918 it was proposed at a meeting of the board of directors to "secure notes from customers whose accounts were more than one year over-due." Here is evidence of the revival of one of the bad habits that the Co-operative was designed in 1882 to correct. Some of it lingers on in 1942, but I believe it is watched with the greatest of care. In 1915 a decisive step was taken in the initiation of the policy of paying 2 per cent lower dividends on all charge sales. The purpose of this was partly to meet the cost of handling the charge accounts and perhaps partly also to discourage the whole charge business. I see no reason why the differential should not be 3 per cent.

President Munro was conscious of the fact that the Society owed much of its success to the faithful work of its employees. Moreover, he had a feeling of social responsibility, or of justice if you will. The whole matter of employee relations was considered during most of the year 1914. After business hours on December 10, 1914, the staff was called together, apparently for the first time in the history of the Society. A new profit-sharing plan was explained and probably approved by the employees. The bonus system was changed from a rate according to salary to equality within the department; in other words, the bonus was put upon a departmental basis of performance. The board of directors had previously recorded its desire to admit "employees to some benefit from increases in the business of the various departments," and, we may add, to encourage employees not only to be courteous to customers but to be effective in selling. Since there had been some problems connected with the charge accounts of employees, it was decided in 1915 to sell to employees at cost only when cash was paid. In 1917 a bonus was voted to "lower paid employees" to the extent of 10 per cent of their wages and to certain heads of departments to the extent of 5 per cent. This bonus was to meet the high cost of living, resulting from war conditions. In 1919 it was stated in a board meeting that the honesty of employees was greater in some departments than in others, and best in departments where the clerks were of long service. Only one clerk had been discharged for dishonesty in the last six months. At the close of the period under consideration the superannuation fund was being discussed, and indeed in 1918–19 the Employees' Reserve Fund made its beginning in the annual statements.

Clearly, the Society had never had a president that cut so deeply into policy and management as did Professor Munro. No one ever went so far to develop administration or to get "outside business." His was the vision of catering to distant alumni, that flared up only to fade away. Even a leased department for the sale of flowers was maintained for a period in 1913 and in a short time seemed to be profitable, for the Society received 20 per cent of the sales which amounted to $1,200. Since this department did not maintain its early promise, however, it was dropped. The records are full of plans and experiments, many of which succeeded.

President Munro found it necessary to stimulate his board of directors: he invited the directors over to the old Colonial Club. Their meetings in the superintendent's office had been haphazard and casual. He prepared an agendum and called for incisive action. He asked for and got reports from the officers. He asked the stockholders to increase the fees paid to the directors from $2.00 to $2.50 for each attendance. When he became president after the War, he was responsible for raising the fee to $5.00; and he still remembers the look on the faces of the undergraduate members of the board when the treasurer handed around the shiny gold pieces in that golden age of the past. In some cases, these bits of gold were the first earnings of the undergraduates. The sum for attendance has not changed but the payment is now in paper.

During Professor Munro's presidency, the stockholders were none too active. Their meetings were largely routine. The ticket-holders received only official neglect. The average attendance at the annual meetings of the ticket-holders, 1903–19, was five, chiefly officers and other directors. Perhaps this was a serious fault in President Munro's policy — not to keep alive the participation of ticket-holders (members) in the direction of the Society's affairs. No, he was not going in the direction of democracy but of administrative efficiency — the effective operation of the Society by an executive committee made up of officers, of whom the most important was ultimately to be the superintendent. It was President Munro who laid the foundations for the deep guidance of an able superintendent.

§2. Superintendents follow fast, 1911–1915. During the period 1903–42 there were only three superintendents — Laws, Goodwin, and Cole. On the other hand, during the three years 1911–14 these same three were following one another fast. Laws has already been considered for the period 1903–06. During that period he did not seem a success in the eyes of the directors. Things changed for Laws, however, when Professor Munro became president in 1906. Just why is hard to determine. In 1908 it was reported that there had been a marked increase in the usefulness of Mr. Laws "in the past two years." Accordingly, he was given a higher salary ($3,000) and a five-year contract. I surmise that President Munro learned how to work with Laws to the Society's benefit. In 1911 Laws resigned to take a position in a department of a large manufacturing concern, as we have already observed. From the standpoint of salary, this may have been an advance, but from the standpoint of executive grade and challenge to leadership it was a distinct retrogression. Hardly anything could throw more light on Laws than this change. When he left, however, he was given the usual vote of "loyalty and efficiency;" his outstanding personal achievement consisted in bringing about a better understanding between the Co-operative and the other business firms at Harvard Square.

The head of the furniture department — M. H. Goodwin — was made acting superintendent (at $1,800 in 1911) and later superintendent. This was the second time a superintendent had been taken from the ranks of the Society's own staff, the first being Thomas, head of the Medical Branch. Appointed on the strong recommendation of Laws, Goodwin was clearly incapable of advancing along the lines of merchandising control or creative selling. As early as 1912, an outsider was considered as expense manager and at once, as we have seen, Mr. George E. Cole was brought in to fill the office. Goodwin proved incapable of managing either the store or his own personal finances. When in 1914 he mixed his own and the store's funds, there was nothing to do but to let him go.

The third of the superintendents of this period — the sixth in the history of the Society — was Mr. George E. Cole, whom we have already noted and whose work we shall have occasion to examine in the next chapter. Mr. Cole's success as expense manager and managing director during 1912–14 was outstanding. In 1914 he was given a leave of absence, as we have seen, and in his new job learned all that business should not be. When invited back as superintendent in 1915, he had had less than two years of business experience since leaving college. But Mr. Cole is quick and learns with lightning rapidity. Indeed, by 1915 he was at Hanover for two days, explaining to Dartmouth leaders how to conduct a co-operative. During the same year he prepared the budget for 1915–16, that is, he was already in effective charge. It was fortunate that a quick learner and an incisive man was entering the business, because President Munro, busy with other tasks, was anxious to have someone else take over the burden. Nothing is more noticeable than that Mr. Cole succeeded Professor Munro, not in the presidency but in general leadership even in 1915–17. This situation is reflected in the boost of salary which the new superintendent received, roughly, if not exactly, as follows:

SALARY OF MR. GEORGE E. COLE

1913 — $1,500	1916 — $4,000
1914 — 1,800	1917 — 5,000
1915 — 2,600	1918 — 8,000

These rapid increases came partly because of the clear recognition of the new superintendent's ability as a manager of men and situations and also partly because other opportunities were being offered him to go elsewhere. It is doubtful whether the Society had ever had a superintendent whom other business men were eager to employ. A new managerial situation was at hand.

§3. The Co-operative branches out. The Harvard Co-operative Society has had a rich experience in establishing branches, as the following list indicates.

BRANCHES OF THE HARVARD CO-OPERATIVE SOCIETY

Location	Established	Discontinued
Medical School	1896(?)	1903
Thurston's at the Square	1909	1920
Technology	1916	....
Plattsburgh, N. Y.	1917	1918
School of Business	1927	....

Branch stores have been established in America here and there since the seventeenth century. Department stores were being formed into branch or chain systems during this very period of the Co-operative's activity. The Co-operative Society was not at all out of line.

The stationery store of C. H. Thurston at 1322 Massachusetts Avenue (very near the second site of the Society's Main Store) was on the market early in 1909. The watchful President — Munro — saw that the Society might be needing a second store in view of the fact that the Boston Elevated Company had plans for constructing a subway right under the Main

Store in Lyceum Hall. The alterations would disrupt business for a period and might even take the whole basement. Moreover, the Society's business was growing and another outlet seemed promising. The Society could handle "a strictly high grade stationery store" so conveniently located as Thurston's. As time went on, other services might be performed such as the selling of theater tickets (by 1913), phonograph records, and even cigarettes, tobacco, and cigars (1919). As early as 1915, however, this Harvard Square Branch proved unprofitable in so far as it did not bear its fair share of the overhead costs of business, but it was recognized to have advertising value and to be convenient for the members. After doing an annual business between $20,000 and $30,000, the store was discontinued in 1920. The Co-operative found out for itself, what had been demonstrated in 1909, that a specialized stationery store could not succeed at Harvard Square.

The Plattsburgh Branch was for the convenience of members attending the officers' training camp. It had to do largely or wholly with providing uniforms. The chief branch — the one at the Massachusetts Institute of Technology — is really a second store and deserves special consideration. The last branch — at the School of Business — is really more like a root than a branch, for it is underground. Long, narrow, and crowded, it at least has perspective which, however, leads only to the barbershop. But the boys like it and the store thrives.

§4. The Technology Store. The Massachusetts Institute of Technology had apparently set up a co-operative society in 1886, that is, while it was still in Boston. At that time the Institute had only 637 students and these students did not live in a closely nucleated dormitory group. Accordingly, it was more practical to follow the plan, apparently in effect at the University of Toronto at least as early as 1882, namely, of agreeing to buy from an existing store at a favorable rate. When we come to the period of 1914–16, when the Institute was moving from Boston to Cambridge, the Technology Co-operative Society was functioning largely through a book and stationery store kept by a former Technology student, A. D. Maclachlan, of the class of 1896. This man was selling to all-comers at the going prices and giving to all students who could show a membership in the Technology Co-operative Society a discount of 10 per cent. He seems to have been moderately successful and to have got a lot of satisfaction out of helping Technology students. He went as far as to arrange with other retailers in Boston to give Technology students belonging to the Society a discount on their purchases. When the move to Cambridge became known, Maclachlan could see no great opportunity in following the Institute across the River where he could have very little business except that of the members of the Technology Co-operative Society — at a discount of 10 per cent.

According to information given me by the then secretary of the M.I.T. Alumni Association, Mr. Walter Humphreys, there were three alternatives before the Institute. It might persuade Maclachlan, against his will, to move his store to Cambridge. It could set up a fresh store through its Technology Co-operative Society, hitherto little more than a buying pool. Or, it could ask to have a Harvard Co-operative branch established near at hand. There was much in favor of the third course and it was the one chosen. The Institute and Harvard were co-operating financially and intellectually. Moreover, the Harvard Co-operative was a going mercantile organization which, under Munro, was adding success to success. Accordingly, in 1914, on the initiative of Major (later Colonel) Edwin T. Cole, U. S. A., professor of Military Science at the Institute, who was then greatly interested in undergraduate affairs, and in hearty co-operation with a special committee appointed by the Technology Alumni Council, the officers of the Harvard Co-operative Society began to consider the matter of a branch at the Institute. Dr. R. C. Maclaurin, president of the Institute, joined in making this request. In the same year, an agreement to establish a branch was entered into with the understanding that members of the Institute might become members of the Harvard Co-operative Society and share in dividends and in the administration of the Society. In 1916 the Harvard Co-operative Society purchased at least part of the stock in trade of Maclachlan, who agreed not to compete with the Harvard Co-operative Society.

A store was set up in a rented block, the building of which was made possible, financially, by the Society's willingness to take a long lease. Within a few doors a barbershop was opened. In fact during the War, in connection with the canteen in Technology buildings, a second barbershop was established. Remember that the place where Technology settled in Cambridge, between the River and the railroad tracks, was not a shopping center and, except for large apartment houses overlooking the River, there were few residences in the district. The convenience of the store and the barbershop was obvious, though neither was universally appreciated. Deeds proved louder than words, however, for the Branch did a business of $84,349 during the very first year.

At first there were no charge accounts at the Technology Branch owing to the opposition of President Maclaurin of the Institute, who was firmly convinced that students should be discouraged from buying on credit; accordingly, only one rate of dividend was declared on purchases. By 1919, however, differential dividends were in force at the Institute and by 1920 the same rates as were paid to the Harvard group, namely 10 per cent for cash and 8 per cent for charge sales, were paid to the Technology members. The question remains open whether the Technology Store should have its own dividend rate, determined by its own earnings. By 1937 a fine new store building was finished and occupied. It contained the store and storehouse, a barbershop and a luncheonette. Before the building was completed, somebody painted across the front of the store and in large letters, "Tech Is Hell." This is an affectionate translation of the Institute's motto, *Mens et Manus*.

The Technology Store, for such is the local name, is a real merchandising branch of the Harvard Co-operative Society and an integral part of the Society's financial structure. The investment in land and building has been heavy (about $90,000). Already the accommodation is overcrowded — a fact which gives the Store an untidy appearance. The Institute's representatives (students, alumni, faculty, and administrators) have been and are strong and influential in the Society's affairs. From the first, there has been an unsettled position in the matter of the equity of the Institute's members. The legal position is clear: the residual claim to the Society's assets, in case of dissolution, rests in the Harvard group. Quite in accordance with their mature and considered opinion, the Institute's early representatives and negotiators, recognizing the situation, let it pass on the ground that action by the Harvard members of the Society would be difficult to obtain. And so it happens, year after year, that part of the net profits of the Technology Store are added to the capital and surplus of the Harvard Co-operative Society, though earmarked as the surplus of the Technology Store. So long as the Society continues as at present, there can be little question about this arrangement; nevertheless, if Technology representatives in the administration of the Society should call for more emphasis on dividends and less on addition to capital and surplus, it would be difficult for a third party to avoid sympathizing with the policy. Certainly, as conditions are at present, any such policy would receive careful consideration by the board of directors and the (board of) stockholders.

All in all, I wonder whether the time has not come to change the name from the Harvard Co-operative Society to the College Co-operative Society and to make other adjustments to correspond with the new conditions. The way for such action has been gradually opened up — in 1887, 1902, and following — when participating membership was thrown open to non-Harvard groups. So long as fat dividends are available and services are satisfactory and so long as no alternative organization is in sight, the existing arrangements will doubtless hold. At present, the Institute clearly recognizes the advantage it has had in being able to utilize the administrative and managerial set-up of the Society and, so far as I know, the Institute's representatives are well satisfied, but time may level off this feeling of content. The Harvard sentiment connected with the loss of the name Harvard in the title would wear off in a decade. What may count may be a solid broad basic organization of persons in a position to uphold rights established and well justified. Although we may not see the point very clearly now, circumstances may demonstrate that it is a wise policy to recognize facts inside and outside: the Society is no longer an exclusively Harvard institution.

§5. Just mishaps. On the whole, the Co-operative Society has fared rather well in a world of chance; but, then, Harvard Square is a protected zone and little mischance arises there. And yet we do have to record some mishaps.

On Christmas Eve, 1909, the water main broke in front of Lyceum Hall, the Society's store building. The basement was flooded and vast quantities of stationery and other goods stored there were ruined, besides the floors and fixtures. In less than two months the Metropolitan Water and Sewerage Board paid for the damages to the amount of $13,333.84.

Then, in 1910, the Boston Elevated Company planned to extend its subway right under one corner of Lyceum Hall. Even though the subway might be run beneath the basement rather than through it, still the Society was greatly inconvenienced and made to suffer from some loss of business. To this day, the rumble of subway trains is a bit disconcerting to the customer looking for dolls or kiddy cars in the basement. The Society claimed just under $20,000 for easement and damages in 1912, but late in 1913 accepted about half that amount, which was promptly used to reduce the mortgage on the Society's real estate.

The destruction and replacement of the old Lyceum Hall had long been planned, and reserves had been set aside to meet the costs; but the European War, breaking out in 1914, put an end to plans for demolition and reconstruction. In the meantime, the fire god tried his hand — on May 12, 1918. A little before 3:30 A.M. a Harvard watchman who lived near the rear of the store, wakened by smoke or crackling glass, put in an alarm, which, however, did not register. A second effort brought the firemen in full clanging force, only to face the whole third floor and roof ablaze. The firemen did what they could to cover up merchandise on the lower floors, but the water and smoke caused a good deal of damage, even where the fire never reached. Luckily for the Store, the records were unharmed. Within a week after the fire, the insurance companies settled with the Society for $26,200 and the directors were appeased with the fire god.

What caused the fire is not clear. Since it broke out in the workshop of the tailoring department, some persons concluded that the pressing irons had been left uncared for. Or perhaps there was some faulty wiring — the easy explanation when all other guesses fail. Some time before, careful attention had been given to an automatic sprinkling system. Now, it was possible to argue definitively that the Society should have a new and fire-proof building, which it actually got only in 1925.

Doubtless there was great disappointment among the student body slumbering in the Yard and in the new dormitories along the River, not because the store had escaped complete destruction but because the fire was over by 5:50 in the morning. There is no time in the day when students are so dead to the world as the very hours the fire occurred — on a Sunday morning! And so, the firemen had to fight the conflagration without benefit of collegiate support or advice.

The store had been badly messed up, and the superintendent and staff had a real job of reorientation ahead of them. Within three days, however, the store was open for some kind of business on the same site. Within eight days the superintendent announced a Fire Sale and then a Smoke and Water Sale. The fire having been liquidated and the stock watered, the store resumed its work for posterity.

President Munro was the one who was living through *all* these troubles. He must have philosophized about the tricks that fate plays on the best and most carefully managed houses. When America entered the War in 1917, a larger and more lasting mischance arrived. Within one month, the University authorities announced that they expected a loss of from 30 to

40 per cent of the student body the next year. Actually, the drop in attendance was from 5,656 in 1916–17 to 3,684 in 1917–18. The corresponding change in the Society's membership was a drop from 5,035 (including Technology) to 3,871. In 1917–18 there were reduced sales and very reduced net profits, so that there was less for dividends and much less available for addition to capital and surplus.

Business was still living in a price economy during the war years, 1917–18, in contradistinction to the regulated economy begun in 1933. In the early period, prices went up when scarcity threatened and down when demand was likely to slacken. The system was self-regulatory. True, the poor could not buy so much of all the things they needed, but in the first World War the workers were so well paid that they could buy luxuries at high prices. The business man had to watch his step and build up his fences. The Society's aim was to stock up in 1917–18, especially in staples, but to avoid being caught at the end of the War with goods bought at high prices. Though difficult to carry out, this policy was clear cut. The goods in stock varied as to prices: although stationery and furniture were stocked at a low price, shoes and shirts were high. Accordingly, only a few of the latter were stocked. The prices of goods were marked up, so as to yield a greater gross margin of profit which was needed to make up for an anticipated loss when prices would fall after the War. Reserves against depreciation of merchandise doubled in the four years 1916–19, inclusive. When in 1920 the drop in prices actually began, the Society had built up its reserves much higher still. It had played safe. Although Professor Munro had gone into war work in 1918–19, returning in a major's uniform, he became president of the Society again in 1920 and 1921, in other words just in time to participate in the primary post-war reaction. The Society had been decreasing its stock and building up its reserves. It had become cautious and now had no financial difficulty. In fact, while there was a dip in dividend rates in 1917 and 1918, there was declared in 1920 the highest rate of dividend yet attained, one, in fact, not surpassed till 1940.

And so, fire, flood, and war came and went. The Society kept on — adding to its services, increasing its dividends, buying more real estate, and building up its capital and surplus.

§6. Results of operation, 1906–1919. Throughout this period the annual report of the Society may be studied in printed pamphlets. The reports were at first quite full and explanatory. Gradually, from about 1912, they became briefer and less explicit — a tendency that has increased unfortunately down to the present. Well, anyone with a flair for accounting statements and business statistics is invited to read these reports for himself. Some of the tables printed in the appendices in this book have been in part taken from these reports.

One outstanding fact is that the Society's business just about doubled during this period. Part of this increase came from the Technology Store. The stationery department showed the greatest growth, with furniture, men's furnishing, and book departments coming along behind. The tailoring department actually experienced a loss in business. All this is part of the seesaw in internal business conditions, watched so closely by the superintendent and the board of directors. Remember always that the Society's store is really an aggregation of little stores, called departments, which the superintendent has to keep working together effectively.

Expenses changed but little in percentage of sales' volume. Net profits made little or no absolute increase after 1909–10, being at their lowest rate in 1913–14 and 1914–15. This suggests what John Claflin in New York and retailers generally were finding: it was becoming increasingly difficult to make profits in retailing. This was also found in American and European business as a whole. It is an interesting suggestion that fear that the business recession would lead to a major depression, even to a turn in the secular trend in prices and business, really led to the World War of 1914–18. The idea was that a war would prevent a serious economic depression. At any rate, the Society was experiencing its share of world-wide difficulties.

The net profits from operation were used to pay dividends

and to add to capital and surplus. The old rule that two-thirds of net profits should go to dividends and one-third to capital and surplus did not survive the reorganization and the purchase of real estate in 1903. There has been a marked tendency to try to pay a dividend rather close to last year's, preferably even at a little higher rate. During the last two years of this period, indeed, dividends were kept up (or not dropped over one per cent) at the expense of "addition to capital and surplus." How far this was a concession to Technology, which had just come into the Society, is not clear.

For land and buildings, nothing had been spent till 1903. Since that time, this non-current asset has been a heavy item in the Society's balance sheet. And for a time borrowings became the order of the day. The treasurer's report, becoming since 1903 an important item in the agenda of the board of directors, usually contained information concerning borrowing sums of money or paying off loans. At first, there was a feeling for a policy of regular depreciation of the value of land and buildings; but, as a matter of fact, the item of real estate was increased, more land being bought near the store in 1913 and 1921, and in 1925 the item of $82,000 for real estate was increased to $405,-000 on the rebuilding of the store. Next year, it was $476,000; and, when the Technology land was purchased and the store building erected, the item had become (by 1937) $570,705.

There is no doubt that the heavy investment in real estate for a time made the Society short of working capital. Many a family has found itself in this situation. Financing was through mortgages and recurring notes. Monthly borrowings at the Harvard Square banks were common. Finally, in 1916 the board of directors planned an issue of preferred stock ($50,000) to provide the necessary working capital for the Technology Store and to use in acquiring more real estate. Since there were technical difficulties in issuing such stock bearing a rate of dividend of over 5 per cent and since it would be difficult to get authorization from the members of the Society, the plan was abandoned the same year in favor of an issue of debenture bonds, which the Cambridge Trust Company floated to the extent of $20,000 without any cost to the Society. These debentures were gradually reduced to $4,000 in 1925, but the new building program of that year boosted them again, this time to $42,000.

When we compare the current assets (cash, merchandise, and accounts receivable) with the current liabilities (accounts payable, customers' deposits, and notes payable), we find only a fair situation for a number of years. The ratio of current assets to current liabilities was between 2 to one and 3 to one. In 1916–17, however, the ratio was increased somewhat; and in both 1917–18 and 1918–19 it was put and kept at 6.6 to one. In other words, when the danger point of the War had been reached, the liquidity was strengthened. It is curious to note that Treasurer McInnes (1903–11) had little consciousness of the difference between current and non-current assets and liabilities. Treasurer Taylor (1911–40) at once made the distinction in his balance sheets but he kept inventory out of the current assets until 1916. The Society's treasurers, being preoccupied with Harvard's finances, which were their principal concern, were not closely keyed up to the importance of transitory financial matters.

It is difficult to find anything about President Munro's administration to criticize. We have already noted that President Munro and his fellow policy-formulators seemed ready to allow the ticket-holders to become inactive and their annual meeting to become moribund. "What the Society needed at that stage," as Professor Munro has recently stated, "was management, initiative, and leadership rather than town-meeting democracy." Of course, this feeling was general and was reflected in current business practice: the stockholders or owners of a business might safely be neglected. But nearer to the subject matter of this section are two possible criticisms, namely, the threatened depletion of working capital in favor of real estate and the low ratio of current assets to current liabilities until corrected by threatening war conditions.

In a general way we may say that, whilst the Society had been in the hands of petty capitalists for many years from its foundation, about 1903 it entered the ranks of industrial capitalism. It was incorporated and given a strong administrative set-up, and the mechanism of efficient accounting control was developed. Like the industrial capitalist, the Society also turned to an emphasis on fixed assets in the form of real estate. It expanded its business and had to borrow at the banks and issue bonds to provide working capital. It was always alarmed at the possible consequences of a panic and depression and had to build its fences hurriedly when trouble threatened. Without knowing it, President Munro was the embodiment of the industrial capitalist, who in the country at large had really been yielding leadership to financial capitalism, especially during the period 1893–1913–1929. It was financial capitalism that commonly corrected the industrial capitalist's weaknesses, such as an undue emphasis on fixed capital resources, inadequate working capital, and frequent borrowing at the commercial banks. We shall see not a little of financial capitalism enter the Society with Mr. Henry S. Thompson, whose presidency began in 1922 and is described in the next chapter.

CHAPTER V

PROSPERITY AND STABILITY, 1919–1942

THE MANAGER STEERS THE SHIP

§1. George E. Cole — the man and the manager. Mr. Cole has had a longer experience in the affairs of the Society than any other man, except President Thompson — just about half the Society's existence. In that time, he has learned to steer the ship and he never misses a harbor.

Mr. Cole was born in Holyoke, Massachusetts, October 24, 1888. His boyhood was not particularly eventful. During the summers he worked in his father's machine-shop as a relief from school; but in September he went back to school as a relief from the machine-shop. After doing this for four years, at the age of 20, he decided to go to college. Having been graduated from Clark College in 1911, he attended the Harvard School of Business for one year, 1911–12. During the year he obtained a scholarship, for which, at a later date, he reimbursed the School. In his work he stood in the top-third of the class. Then, from June to November, 1912, he was employed in Filene's store in Boston. On the strong recommendation of Professor Gay, dean of the School of Business, he was chosen by President Munro as expense manager of the Society — in November, 1912. His first impressions of the Co-operative were that the stock was excessive in amount, the turnover was slow, and personal relations were strong. In other words, there was a great need for inventory-control and for what is called institutionalization.

Mr. Cole is short in stature but long in energy. In performance his score is high. He is thoroughly alive and alert to all about him. He speaks with rapidity and his ideas come too fast for ordinary utterance. He does more than manage the

GEORGE E. COLE IN 1942, SUPERINTENDENT 1915–19
MANAGER SINCE 1919

store: he lives it. He does two or three men's work and prefers not to have an understudy. Temperamentally, he works best alone — or with only assistants. He has the business in such a shape that the Society could run along for three or four months on its own momentum. During this period there would be ample time for securing a successor.

Although open to suggestion, Mr. Cole is essentially conservative. Proud of his job, he is ready to admit his mistakes and he has made some, though they have not been serious.

In January, 1922, when Professor Munro was resigning from the presidency of the Society, he recommended "that the Board [of directors] depend upon the advice of its Manager." This was a strong legacy and over the years it has proved to be a gold mine for the Society. But, in fact, as Mr. Cole points out, the board of directors often refuses to follow his advice, as I have myself observed. Nevertheless, Mr. Cole's statements and opinions win so often because they are close to reality, whilst the board's existence is so remote from the daily round of the Society's affairs. The man who knows is the man who should prevail. Mr. Cole apparently resents the implication that "this is Cole's Store:" he claims it is just the place where he works. But, as early as 1923, one director said in a board meeting "that the organization is a one man concern." President Thompson promptly denied this. But still the president and the whole board have sealed the issue by raising Mr. Cole's salary. Undoubtedly, Mr. Cole could earn much more than his present salary in the big stores of Boston or New York. He has had no increase since 1929, and during the depression he insisted on a reduction.

Here is a major point to remember. Since 1903 the chief problem of the Society has been management. Dean Donald K. David, of the School of Business, who was a director during the period 1921–26, has made this clear, and the records of the Society amply corroborate the point. Mr. Cole is the management, that is all. But, then, this fact may create a problem some day when the time comes for choosing a successor.

Although an individualist in the sphere of management, Mr.

Cole is really most co-operative — with the executive committee, the board of directors, the (board of) stockholders, and the
members. Obviously, he does not use the power that is born of
competence and results in success. Perhaps he is too wise to be
vain; or perhaps he knows that external situations may at any
time turn his black ink into red and his gold into ashes.

Mr. Cole loves a deal, but he wants to be sure that he can see
how the other fellow will profit from the transaction. Thus, he
is a genuine "economic man" in the best sense. His aim is to
serve and to profit from service. It follows that he would please
his customers and treat his staff fairly. He keeps abreast of the
time, partly by attending the meetings of business men who are
wrestling with problems similar to his own. While he is concerned with every aspect of the business, he is directly responsible for the making of net profits. As we shall see, others are
more immediately charged with long-time finances and legal
matters. Perhaps the central policy that he unconsciously follows is to emphasize the profitable part of available business.
This is good business policy, good private business policy, and
probably that is why it has succeeded so well with the Co-
operative. I do not imply that this policy will hold indefinitely,
but it appears to be good for a few years to come.

§2. Stability through long service. Although no one else
matches Mr. Thompson's 32 years of service or Mr. Cole's 30
years, still there are others who are not so far behind. As it
seems to me, the record is noteworthy.

Mr. Walter Humphreys has been a member of the board of
directors since 1917 and the secretary since 1918. After experience as an engineer, Mr. Humphreys became registrar of
the Massachusetts Institute of Technology in 1902, a post which
he held till 1922. He taught in Mechanical Engineering and
during the last two years of this period held the rank of associate professor. From 1906 to 1923 he was secretary-treasurer
of the Alumni Association of the Institute. Since 1922 he has
been secretary-treasurer of the National Association of Wool
Manufacturers and since 1929 a life member and secretary of

the Technology Corporation. Obviously the Harvard Co-operative is fortunate in having a man of such experience. Mr. Humphreys is not a mere recorder, though he does know his records. He has an unusual capacity for formulating votes and therein exerts considerable influence. He is prompt and decisive. He has a strong urge to get along with the business at hand.

Professor Austin W. Scott, of the Harvard Law School, has been vice-president of the Harvard Co-operative since 1922. After the withdrawal of Vice-President Schaub in 1921 there was great need for an officer well versed in business law. Professor Scott has been the legal adviser for many years, and recently has been regularly retained as counsel. The manager finds more and more that he needs to consult the vice-president on legal matters. Not only is his advice useful in making contracts but also in dealing with national and State price legislation, matters of tax liabilities (State and federal), pensions, social security, and trusteeship. In a sense, Professor Scott represents, or is reminiscent of, the old régime (before 1906), in which the Law School provided the leading group in the administration of the Society. Professor Scott believes that the Society's organization for controlling the board of directors through the (board of) stockholders works very well. He sees the undergraduate members of the board getting an education in business administration, though the number is very small. He is pleased to see the Society now carrying some lower-priced goods.

Since 1923, Dr. A. C. Redfield, professor of Physiology, has been a member of the board of directors. He has a lot of common sense and experience, which are of great value in weighing the issues presented.

Mr. Delmar Leighton (A.B. '19), director since 1923, studied at the School of Business for two years, receiving the degree of M.B.A. in 1922. The same year he became assistant-dean of Harvard College and now is dean of Freshmen. His combination of training in business and knowledge of the undergraduate group and its needs constitutes a valuable asset to the Society.

Somebody must make suggestions as to the most likely students to be considered for membership on the board of directors. Dean Leighton is in a fine position to help in this. It is to be expected that he would be interested in the educational aspects of the Co-operative's work. Indeed, his interest along this line was one of the influences that led to the writing of the present volume.

Professor Kenneth B. Murdock (A.B. '16), of the department of English, has been a director since 1927. A Scottish ancestry, a family tradition of banking, a long preoccupation with New England puritanism, an experience in academic administration, and a native shrewdness make Professor Murdock an invaluable director.

Mr. Carroll L. Wilson (Technology '32) exemplifies a type of continuity which is worthy of every encouragement. Mr. Wilson was a student-director, 1931–32. Then, since 1936, he has been a director at large, chosen from Technology alumni. After graduation, Mr. Wilson was assistant to the president of the Massachusetts Institute of Technology. Then, he became an executive in the Research Corporation. Whether it is because he comes of a family long interested in accounting or because he has native executive ability, he has been a useful member of the board of directors.

One cannot help asking why so many men continue to serve the Society so long. The officers are paid salaries and the directors fees, but these are quite inadequate to compensate them for their time and effort. They just like the Society and enjoy being useful. We may note, however, that beneficent institutions and firms (such as Harvard and Technology and the National Association of Wool Manufacturers) make possible this service to the Society by a policy of not exacting too much effort from their employees. The Society is the beneficiary of other institutions' liberality. In spite of President Munro's insistence that the Society be a business and not a charity, there is an element of charity in the service of its functionaries.

Anyone who has served on an executive committee knows that it ordinarily takes from three to five years to become intimately acquainted with the procedures and problems. After a few years the individual can see through certain situations very quickly and incisively. Moreover, he can recall success and failure and steer accordingly. In short, he brings continuity and with continuity stability.

All this is good, but there comes a time in the holding of every office when continuity gives way to routine and stability to stagnation. This leads to the question how long a man should continue as an executive or a director. There is no answer.

§3. The decemvirate — the (board of) stockholders. The constitutional provisions of 1902 and the by-laws of 1903 provided for 5 (later 10) stockholders who were to hold the stock (500 shares of $100 each) in trust for all the members. The outstanding function of the stockholders is not to hold stock but to nominate and elect the officers and other directors of the Society. Only current or present officers and students of Harvard University have an alternative right to vote for officers and other directors of the Society. (And they, along with members from Radcliffe, would have the sole right to vote, if the corporation were to be dissolved and the Society should go back to the original condition of an unlimited partnership.) Under existing circumstances the stockholders exercise great, though limited, powers. Each holds office for 5 years, 2 being elected or re-elected annually on an average.

Over a period of 40 years, 1902–42, there have been 40 stockholders, who have had an average period of service of over 8 years. Indeed, there are 7 stockholders with an average of nearly 18 years. During the earliest years Professor (and Dean) Wallace C. Sabine was a most helpful member — till his death in 1919. Professor Chester N. Greenough served 23 years from 1915 to his death in 1938. Dean Wallace B. Donham has been a stockholder since 1920 and, if he continues in office till the end of his present term, he will have served for 26 years. Indeed, the list of stockholders is a brass tablet of distinguished names — A. Lawrence Lowell, Edwin F. Gay, Felix Frankfurter, Davis R. Dewey, and many others.

An analysis of the occupations of the present stockholders shows that 4 are deans, one a librarian, 3 professors, one a director of physical education, and one a non-faculty administrator. Seven are from Harvard, 2 from Technology, and one from Radcliffe. These 10 men serve without pay, hold without holding, and own without owning. Twice a year they have their regular meetings — in September and October. In spite of the reported excellence of the food, the attendance is only about 3 to 7, for the stockholders are busy men. Besides the stockholders, there come together at these meetings such officers of the Society as are free at the time. The secretary of the Society is the clerk of the stockholders, and the president of the Society presides. At their meetings the affairs of the Society are ably and wisely discussed.

In recent years the stockholders have held a spring meeting at which the prospects for a dividend and the general policies of the Society have been discussed. This is one of the bits of evidence that the stockholders are developing a greater interest in the general affairs of the Society. To further these interests they have appointed committees to report on various items of business. We cannot help contrasting this situation with the meeting in which Dean Haskins was the only stockholder present, the other nine functioning through proxies. But then, this was during the war year 1918.

The ten trustees nominate and then elect the officers and other directors, as we have seen, except that the board of directors chooses the manager. (Technically, they just nominate the president but the board of directors has the duty of electing their nominee.) The presence of a Harvard and a Technology dean helps them in choosing undergraduate directors or in considering those suggested by the existing board.

There is reason for not accepting this constitutional picture as wholly accurate except in form. In reality, the very efficient officers of the Society, especially the manager, president, and treasurer, are in a position to make recommendations concerning policies and actions, nominations and elections, which are so well considered that wisdom indicates that the stockholders should merely confirm. So long as such leadership prevails, the stockholders have an easy time. If existing leadership should fail, however, then the stockholders would proceed to seek more efficient officers. Thus, the routine nature of the stockholders' work is a tribute to their effectiveness.

The normal working of the administrative mechanism seems to be something like the following. One of the officers — the president or the manager — makes a suggestion in the executive committee; this committee makes a recommendation to the board of directors; and, if the matter is of constitutional or long-time financial import, the recommendation goes up to the (board of) stockholders for final decision. The process may be reversed: a stockholder may stimulate the (board of) stockholders to discuss a general question, which may be passed along to the president for consideration by the board of directors; and, then, before the board of directors is given the problem, the executive committee has reached a point where it can make a definite suggestion or propose an acceptable solution. In truth, the executive committee, made up of paid officers, is influential in the action of both stockholders and directors, for it is a master of detail and a fertile source of new policies.

Thus, we see fluidity of ideas within the administration, just as we see stability. If it were not for the fluidity, then there would be greater danger of stagnation than there is at present. If amending the by-laws is a mark of fluidity, then the stockholders are making their contribution.

Not a few think that this undemocratic form of administration might be widely used in business. Certainly, it works in the Harvard Co-operative, in spite of the warning that it is dangerous to put power into the hands of men who do not have ownership. The decemvirs, however, are motivated not by profits but by the desire to see the Society prosper, a Society that is closely connected with the institutions from which they derive their principal support in life. The arrangement in the case of the Society seems sound and safe enough from the mere standpoint of effective administration. Men accustomed to choose subordinate executives are charged with the duty of doing this for the Society. Men who are regularly deciding on policies for their schools or departments are in a position to decide policies for the Society. On the surface, it is as dangerous as a public utility holding-company arrangement; but, in fact, it is as safe as a college administrative committee.

§4. Prosperity, 1919–1942. In the long downward secular trend of prices and business, in which the world is still wallowing (since 1920), it is pleasant to learn of prosperity. We have had occasion before to note that the Co-operative prospers in both good times and bad. If students have money to spend, they readily and conveniently go to the Co-operative to buy books and shoes, typewriters and clothing. If they have less to spend, they still go to the Co-operative to make what they have go farther — through the dividend.

The increase in membership since 1919 has been considerable. A larger percentage of students and faculty members has joined, and there has been an increase in the number of alumni and also unclassified persons (many collegiate employees) putting down their dollar for participating membership. The story that the statistics tell (see Appendix 8) is that not only is there an increase in member-customers but there are still a great many persons qualified for membership who do not join. Here is a problem yet unsolved. Perhaps some of the unaffiliated persons would join, if they could buy shirts as cheaply at the Co-operative as at the bargain basement of a Boston store, that is, if they could buy more goods of a lower quality but still wares of merit, such as many a graduate student, for instance, is forced to be content with.

With the increase in membership has come an increase in sales, the ups and downs of which are indicated as follows:

1919–20	$ 874,111
1929–30	1,394,391
1933–34	938,605
1941–42	1,639,326

These figures do not reflect the business cycles that keep recur-

ring under the New Deal (as under the Old Order) so much as
do the figures for net profits. These net profits may be shown
in skeleton form as follows:

1919–20	$ 40,136
1928–29	105,864
1933–34	55,600
1937–38	106,088
1938–39	88,406
1941–42	186,787

On the surface, one would conclude that the recession of 1938,
which was not reflected in lower sales, was reflected in lower
profits — that is, the same sales at a lower price.

Dividends are most emphasized by the participating members. The rates of annual dividends have varied, though the
trend is upward:

Period	Cash	Charge
1919–20	9	7
1920–32	10	8
1933–35	9	7
1936–39	10	8
1940–	12	10

This dividend record is splendid, but the final judgment must
be deferred until we know whether there will some day be a
serious reduction in the rate, a circumstance that might disas-
trously cut in on the enrollment of members and through this
might affect sales unfavorably.

The over-all growth may be seen in a statement of changes
in assets and liabilities:

1919–20	$ 245,090
1929–30	956,182
1933–34	912,129
1941–42	1,114,784

The Society is out of debt for goods, fixtures, and real estate,
and it holds ample reserves against anticipated contingencies,
carrying a large bank balance. This is a high tribute to both

policy-formulators and manager. The performance has been excellent both in an absolute sense and in comparison with the records of other department stores in a similar general position. There is a strong minority opinion, however, that the directors have piled Pelion on Ossa.

The factors in the growth of the Society may be put down as five in number: policy-formulation, management (including the work of the whole staff), the growth of the patronizing institutions, the business cycle and secular trend, and local competition forcing down prices. The last-named was noticed in 1924 when two men's furnishing stores and two new bookstores were opened at the Square. In the 1930's came a novelty store and in 1940–41 specialty stores carrying women's wares. But how curious is the reversal of price situations! In 1882 the Society was formed to reduce prices below those charged by other stores at Harvard Square. Now, the Society sells at the level of its competitors. When these competitors are chain stores, the competition is indeed keen. And all the greater is the success of the Society when the lower price is met. As we have seen, the Society long ago gave up the policy of reducing prices at the Square to concentrate on making profits at the new level of local prices which it had helped to create.

To be sure, prosperity has come and remains. But note that in business history we find that it induces complacency and engenders competition. This competition may have the wholesome effect of changing policies and bringing about even greater efficiency.

§5. The Main Store in the new building, 1925–present. The directors did a good job in putting up a new building in 1924–25. It is four stories high, made of red brick and trimmed with white limestone — quite Harvardesque. In truth, it is a synthesis of what one sees and what one remembers. Though a composite, the front is not unpleasant. High in the gable-topped façade a clock keeps time with the deity. Four uncarved stones await their heroes — perhaps Kip, Ames, Munro, and Cole — for the names must be short to get on. At last, we stop

MAIN FLOOR IN THE MAIN STORE, 1942

looking and enter the store by a deep, recessive vestibule that is at once a refuge and a rendezvous. On the right we see a tall, somber clerk who can find the goods in the stationery department. Just opposite is one of the many short girls who love to sell fountain pens to budding authors. On the other side of the central counter is a tall girl with a Queen Elizabeth bob, who sells stockings for ladies and collars for men. On through the front of the store we make our way to the book department, but stop at the book table to gaze at the lone Buddha of the Inner Chamber, where sacred relics in the form of fine editions are safely guarded. Having bought a classic work (one of Loeb's) and having thanked God we do not have to read all the journalism served up in book form and heaped up on the hall table, we make our way to the rear exit only to be reassured by a smiling lady with youthful gray hair that all the books we carry are undoubtedly our own.

Next day we enter again by the front doorway, past the four pillars slightly reminiscent of the former building, and stop to look at the prosaic display of blotters, paper, and books in one of the show windows and at the clothes and shoes in the other. We decide to own a pair of such shoes some day. Then on, inside, we turn sharply to the left, surprised to discover an optician who we had thought was a realtor. Then down the steps into the basement — we land on a floor before we get there, and suddenly. No matter, there are tricycles and kiddy cars at hand and toys in the sub-vestibule. But the big body of the basement is full of furniture. We see at once that we have to stop to study the lay-out. We observe some fine cutlery that we have wanted to buy, cutlery that will really cut. There are toasters to burn and a small assortment of the season's furniture. But the radio department attracts our attention. We have been told that the Co-operative was a pioneer in handling radio materials back in the days of crystal sets over twenty years ago. Here we are at the sport goods which we know we shall never need; so we ascend the rear stairs into the book department to see whether a book from our own pen is carried there. Not finding a single copy, we turn to leave again by the rear door —

onto Palmer Street — a lane with crowded warehouses and over-parked cars.

A third visit takes us to the mezzanine or second floor, where the tailoring department and ready-to-wear clothes are located. To find the always accessible manager we must pass the paymaster, Mr. Downey, and the controller, Mr. Comey, who guard the inner office — modest but adequate — which is also the boardroom. This room has a ventilating system so powerful that no over-smoking director can becloud the issues. But the manager — or, as he might be called, the managing director — takes us up to the office on the rear of the third floor. Here is where the large staff keeps track of debts, both good and none too good. From here are mailed the dividend checks — only once a year. Here are the loose-leaf records of the Society, which are destroyed when the law allows. No, we don't want to see the front part of this floor nor the fourth floor, for these are rented out, but we should like to visit the warehouse across the rear lane. We take a short-cut through the tunnel and try to grasp the whole over-stuffed lay-out of goods, packed and unpacked. There's a pressing-room near at hand — a natural source of a nice new warehouse fire, but there are sprinklers everywhere, so we do not discuss the matter.

What a lot of counters, offices, departments, and storehouses in a relatively compact space! And all this is ours — it works for us, keeps what we need, delivers to our doors, and pays us a dividend. Nowhere is there hurry and never a sign of ruffled feelings, except when some assistant professor shows what stuff he is made of or when a housewife telephones for the delivery wagon to call for a suit of clothes to be cleaned and pressed and then goes off for the day.

*   *   *

The big central store houses most of the merchandise owned by the Society. Its warehouse supplies all three stores. On June 30, 1942, the store's inventory of merchandise amounted to $210,674 — a figure that is above normal because of war

NEW TECHNOLOGY STORE, 1937

conditions. Here are also the central services — accounting-office, shipping-room, and tailoring department.

This Main Store has had 66.5 per cent of the total membership, 77.3 per cent of the employees, and makes 76.1 per cent of the sales. It has had the largest percentage of charge and installment sales — 46.7, against 39.4 per cent for the Technology Branch and 43.8 for the School of Business Branch. Of course, its range of goods is broader and the variety, even of staple wares, more extensive. Partly for these reasons, partly because of the attractive display of goods on the first floor, and partly because of the convenience of location for many members of the two branches, it gets a considerable number of sales that would normally go to the branches themselves. This circumstance of buying at three stores complicates accounting, for the records of each store are kept separately. A School of Business member, for example, may receive three dividend checks, if he buys at the Technology Store and the Main Store as well as at his own branch.

§6. The Technology Store, 1937–present. The store building is moderately modernistic and quite striking on the outside. It is a one-storied, low-lying building with attractive entrances and display windows.

Inside, we are not so pleased: at least two stores are crammed into one. There is no longer a tailoring department, but there is a small supply of shoes. Stationery occupies a considerable part of the whole. Highly specialized materials for Technology students are kept. Many of the articles can be selected by the customer from the counter displays. In the book department texts predominate, though general works have been more popular since cheap editions have been stocked.

A bright-looking barbershop with five chairs will attract the unshaven and the unkempt at any time except before examination. Most dissatisfaction arises in this barbershop: not so much that the barbers are unskilled and do not follow directions as that they expect tips. Such conduct is not co-operative!

The lodestone of the Technology Store is the luncheonette

with a counter in the form of an L at which students may drink and eat and turn on toadstool chairs. About 500 persons are served every day. In practice, they select sweet, energizing things and naturally acquire a pleasant impression of the Store. Some hurry off to classes and laboratories; some stroll around to buy a pencil or a new alarm clock; an occasional man takes a long time to finish. When all others have gone, he ventures a question to the waitress. "You are a married woman, aren't you?" "Yes." "Well, can you tell me how long a boy should go with a girl before he kisses her?" Since the waitress has never made public her reply to the boy, it is necessary for any love-lorn to buy at least a sandwich to get the advice.

Mr. Rice, earlier at the Harvard Square store and then at the School of Business Branch, manages the Technology Store with mingled kindness and firmness. He hears complaints and dispels them with the facts. He makes a point of serving Technology graduates, far as well as near. An alumnus in South America has written for stock-market reports and information concerning patents; he cabled to have flowers sent to his father's funeral. A graduate in Russia wrote for eye-glasses. One in Turkey wanted graph paper.

The Store no longer handles theater tickets and it has lost its bus-ticket service. It will send a messenger for books needed by any member. It will take Western Union telegrams for sending, though it does not receive them for delivery. It cashes checks for members.

A member of the class of 1942 at the Institute investigated complaints against the Technology Store in 1941. The results of his inquiry were summed up in a class thesis. Some of the objections are as follows: the name "Harvard Co-operative Society" is not pleasing; it is believed that the Store's prices are higher than those in Boston; the haircuts are not good; the lunch counter is too short; the employees are not well trained; and there is no co-operation in administration. The student investigator concluded that there is a real need for an educational campaign "to improve goodwill and to correct erroneous opinion." The inquiry, though serious, was not exhaustive. It

TECHNOLOGY STORE, MAIN FLOOR, 1937

TECHNOLOGY STORE, LUNCHEONETTE, 1937

was a study of opinion more than of fact. And, yet, a sizable sampling was made of prices and a comparison made with Boston prices — some proved to be higher, some lower, some just the same. The conclusion was that there is no truth in the charge of high prices at this Store, even though circumstances give it something like a monopoly.

The Technology Store has had 26 per cent of the Society's membership and 18 per cent of the employees and has made 19 per cent of the sales. It helps to bear its share of the general overhead costs and has its own surplus account, which varies from year to year. The rates of dividends paid to its members may vary from those paid at the other stores, but since 1919 they have been the same. The Technology Store's great distinction is to have the lowest percentage of charge and installment sales of the three stores.

The Technology Store has some advantages which are not often realized. It enjoys the superior buying power of the Harvard "Branch." It has the stability that comes from the Society's age, experience, and financial strength. It has the oversight of one manager at hand and another at a distance. True, it needs a new floor covering and a second story for comfort; but these and other good things may come in time.

The Co-operative Society in its turn gains from the Technology Store. Its sales and therefore its buying power are increased. Its administration is strengthened by Technology representatives. And, perhaps above all, the educational co-operation of the two institutions is furthered. Thus, after all — in spite of the complaints — the Harvard Co-operative *is* a co-operative society in administration as well as in sharing profits.

§7. School of Business Store in crowded seclusion. Early in 1925 Dean Donham, of the School of Business, raised the question of establishing a branch of the Co-operative in the new buildings to be erected at Soldiers' Field. The Dean had raised the money to put up a magnificent array of buildings on what was still a marsh. Already he could envisage the needs of the expanded School — a library, administrative building, faculty club, students' club, dormitories, refectories, post office, and students' store. The Co-operative had faith in the vision and speedily agreed. In April, 1927, the estimated stock required was put at $9,000 to $10,000, and in August, just after opening, the estimated annual business (exclusive of the barbershop business) was put at $50,000. All this was based on catering to the student body of about 800 members and a faculty and staff together of about 200. Now, it is interesting to observe how the estimates have worked out: the inventory figure is about right and the estimated sales are only a little under the actual performance, which has proved to be $55,830 annually over the last 14 years.

Like the post office, the store is in a basement at the School of Business. Though centrally located, it was not in evidence until 1941 when a sign was erected to disclose its seclusion. Even at that time it was probably only the emergency of war — which brought the R.O.T.C. and the Navy Supply Corps — that led to so un-Harvard a procedure. Long, narrow, and none too bright, the store has the appearance of crowding. Goods are on every hand — there is room for only one long counter. The branch manager, Mr. Hughes, has a cubicle just behind the obliging cashier. From this point he can hear the cash jingle and the coca-cola gurgle — at the refreshment stand. It is a friendly store and carries a lot of articles — from cough drops to textbooks and from letter paper to shirts.

With 7.5 per cent of the members and 8.7 per cent of the employees, this branch has done 4.9 per cent of the business — about all that can be crowded into the narrow corridor of commerce.

When the R.O.T.C. and Navy men arrived in great numbers in 1940, they were given the right to become participating members. Thereupon the branch became a source of supply for uniforms, shirts, and so on: it was in the service. The volume of sales went up, but the profits were modest because prices were kept at the minimum.

Every month the executive committee and the board of directors, sitting in the Main Store, review the statistics of sales and inventory for all three stores. Less often, they consider net profits, surplus, and dividends. In 1934 part of the net profits of the School of Business Branch was carried to the surplus of the Branch as usual, but during the next two years there were not sufficient profits to pay the dividend at the rate justified by the performance of the other two stores. Accordingly, the directors dipped down into the Branch's surplus to pay the desired dividend. Thus we see that the sizable surplus of the Co-operative not only enables it (if the surplus is held sufficiently in cash) to take a discount on purchases from the manufacturers but also to avoid great irregularities in dividend rates.

Back in 1933, when men were still men but were not conscious of it, there was a crisis — the closing of the banks in March. States had declared moratoria, and then came the bank holiday. The Co-operative could not accept checks because they were of no value. It could not actually accept big bills ($20 and $50), which a few students at the School of Business really had, because it would lose all its change. Accordingly, the Branch allowed all customers who could show Bursar's cards to charge merchandise during the period of the emergency. The plan was a complete success — kept sales moving, students happy, and the store active.

Solicitors selling goods and services abound at Harvard University as at other universities, particularly during the opening of the different terms. The School of Business and the local Branch are sorely tried when the number of unauthorized solicitors gets too large or when competition becomes too keen. One student, who had a contract with the Co-operative to take orders for its laundry service, also had an unauthorized sales line of his own, namely, smoking pipes. A student friend of his, who had suits to sell, also unauthorized, seemed to endanger the prospects for laundry and pipes. Accordingly, this man warned his friend that the Co-operative would get after him and he disclosed to the Co-operative that his friend was a solicitor. This student received the degree of Master of Business Administration and in due time became professor of marketing in a western university. I tell the tale as it was told to me.

One sunny September day a laundry solicitor for the Branch donned his palm beach jacket and proceeded to act as porter for incoming students, obligingly carrying their bags up to the rooms and there clinching a laundry contract. A rival solicitor, whose white coat had not yet arrived, stood by the sidewalk as the other fellow walked past with the bags of his prospect. In an audible whisper this rival said, "Will he tip you?" This spilled the contract on the sidewalk. The Branch regarded this as unfair competition but consoled itself with the thought that next time the trick would probably work the other way. And we are left with the query whether such practices illustrate either competitive co-operation or co-operative competition.

§8. Employees who left for fame or stayed at hame. Like every sizable family, the Co-operative has lost some members of its staff, some leaving for careers elsewhere. Professor Robert E. Rogers, once in the book department, became professor of English and History at the Massachusetts Institute of Technology and the author of a series of syndicated newspaper articles on public affairs. In 1931 he affectionately dubbed the Technology Store "the dearest place on earth." Margaret Sullavan came with her sister from Norfolk, Virginia, to serve the Society in the stationery department. Not receiving more than one dollar a week increase in wages, she and her sister left for Hollywood after less than a year's service. Having become active in local theatrical work in Cambridge, she had discovered her real talent. Before leaving the Co-operative, Miss Sullavan told a fellow worker that, if ever she became rich, she would supply the Society's employees with chairs. Miss Sullavan's distinguished acting brought her fame and wealth but her former fellow workers no chairs: some chairs must have come from other sources. A third distinguished émigrée is Miss Frances Davis, once in the book department, whose book entitled *My*

Shadow in the Sun (New York, 1940), some of my readers may
have examined.

A second group of employees consists of the extras who
have to be employed before Christmas and on the opening of
college. Last year, 47 had to be added at the Main Store alone,
to take care of the Christmas trade, while 69 were required on
the opening of college. Many of these extras are the wives of
graduate students. They do their best, but that best is sometimes not good enough. The weakness of the extras is ignorance
of stock and price, inaccuracy, and slowness of action. Many
years ago, the directors considered decentralizing sales on the
opening of college, perhaps selling textbooks at the class-rooms
where they were to be used.

There is no complete record of the number of employees,
except for about the last 20 years. Here are some significant
figures of employees (excluding the manager) for all stores
combined:

1882	1	1927	103
1896	7(?)	1932	97
1906	60	1937	134
1914	80	1942	161
1922	92		

(Beginning in 1922, the figure is for May)

When we examine the work of the employees, we find that
there has been an increase of 72 per cent in the selling force and
an increase of 83 per cent in the non-selling force in a period of
15 years (1926–40). The selling force is handling a smaller
number of transactions per person and the value of the sales per
selling-employee has been diminishing (1932–40). This looks
like an easier time for the employees, unless they are required
to do their selling in a more approved fashion.

In the period 1932–34 there was a pay-cut of 10 per cent, due
to the depression; but in the period 1934–36 half of this was
restored. Thereafter, the pay-cut was wholly removed. In 1935
the minimum wage was put at $17.00 a week.

The Co-operative has never been unionized. The journeyman

tailors, however, have long held membership in a union. There was a strike in the tailoring department lasting about a year, 1920–21, apparently because of a reduction in wages on changing over to a piece-wage basis. In 1933 there was another strike in the same department under the N.R.A. Code. The manager signed an agreement with the union.

Efforts are made to train the employees. In 1921 lectures on salesmanship were provided. And now, regularly, a typed list of rules on how to make sales and how to handle the cash register is given to employees. There are few complicated duties to perform. Some ways, however, are regarded as better than others. For instance, the clerk is told to say, "Is there anything else?," not, "Is that all?"

The clerks of the Harvard Co-operative are confronted with the special task of recording the number of each customer making a purchase. "Have you a number, Sir?" "Yes, 10,311." At once, I disclose my identity, for the School of Business numbers begin with 10,000. If the purchase is for cash and is for 25 cents or more, the number of the purchaser (if he is to get a dividend on the purchase) must be printed on the sales ticket. And what a lot of punching at the cash register to record the high numbers! Yes, it is true that all ticket-holders, like the sands of the sea, are duly numbered. What if I have forgotten my number? This necessitates the clerk's telephoning to the office for the information. But I have insured against that by having mine made perpetual; after having used it a year, I shall not forget it. But there is one objection to this: the perpetual number-holder never gets any unearned increment. Never does he find that he has a fat dividend this year because the holder of his number last year — a rich and reckless fellow — forgot that his number had been changed. The opposite predicament occurs when an absent-minded professor forgets to enroll at the beginning of the new academic year. Then when he hears that the dividend is to be 12 per cent — "My, oh my, I forgot to sign up this year." The tough-minded thereupon petitions for special dividend consideration, sometimes even presenting the cash-register tickets, thereby indicating (without proving) the purchases but, of course, recorded with the wrong number. Then, what is the board of directors to do? Remember the motto: "The customer is always right," even though this one is clearly wrong. One customer was told to wait a year so that the manager might see whether his normal purchases ran so high. Perhaps it is a matter of "social justice" (I must get this phrase into the book at some point) to pay out dividends on such occasions because a few ticket-holders never call for their dividend checks at all or, if they receive them, never cash them. Although the system is convenient for the ticket-holders and satisfactory to the Society, it must appear to the employees at times as a kind of numbers racket.

Several benefits have been provided for employees. In 1922 a group life insurance plan was established through a large joint-stock insurance company and later placed with Massachusetts savings banks. All but 2 employees were included, and the cost to the Society was estimated to be about $500 a year. In 1940 it was being continued, except for those who had retired and reached the age of 65. Thus, on paying a part of the premium, an employee was insured at much less than cost.

In 1932 an employee retirement plan was set up. The employee was admitted to the system without medical examination. He paid 40 per cent of the cost and the Society paid 60 per cent. Retirement came at the age of 60 with a pension. If death arrived first, then the beneficiary received 60 per cent of the total amount paid. If he left, he got what he had contributed with compound interest at 5 per cent.

In 1940 came the employees' loan fund, whereby the Society set aside so much money to loan to employees — "as payments of wages in advance to responsible employees."

Women as employees entered the store in early days apparently through the bookkeeper's and cashier's office. Then, gradually, they were employed as sales assistants. At one time there was public complaint about the pulchritude of one of them, but that was years ago. Much later (in 1916) it was necessary for the stockholders to give formal assent to the employment of women as clerks in certain departments. Today they are an essential group in the staff as a whole — loyal, dependable, intelligent, and pleasant.

At the beginning of the period dealt with in this chapter, there were unfortunate cleavages in the staff of the Main Store. One was along the line of religion. A second was between old and new employees: the older employees resented the incoming of young boys and girls because these youngsters, who were given a good deal of authority, knew little about the store and seemed to have little sense of loyalty. The feeling of injustice and the irritation thus aroused are frequently experienced in a firm and an institution when considerable new blood is brought in. Whether this is all there was to it, I do not know.

Long, faithful, and intelligent service has been common in the Co-operative. From time to time, employees of 25 years' standing have been congratulated and given checks for $100 each. In 1935 the cashier, Miss May J. Wood, died after 31 years of service. Hers were the qualities of "loyalty, devotion and dependability." Few ever imposed bogus checks on such a person, and perhaps few ever joined the Society through her benign influence. In 1942 Mr. H. C. Moriarty died of an illness that overtook him while still at work. He had begun as clerk in the book department in 1905 and in 1913 was made buyer for, and manager of, the department. It was under his guidance that the Society's bookstore became about the second largest in New England and it was through his efforts that thousands of fine volumes were imported from England, to which he made two buying trips. As far back as 1931 he was congratulated and given a check for $100 on attaining 25 years of service. Had he lived another year, he would have been eligible for retirement. A few months before his death, he fondly told me about the students' caricature of him as "Moriarty in Hades," in which he was shown with a bundle of books, but always with too little and too late.

§9. Managerial changes and results, 1919–1942. By constitutional enactment or by custom the manager has come to control inventory, price, and expense, in so far as these things can be controlled. By force of ability he has attained initiative. By dint of inquiry and observation he has gained information. And, by reason of information and judgment he has acquired influence. Everybody but the manager himself would admit all parts of this situation. There is not a little in business history to indicate that a great firm is the lengthened shadow of a great business man.

We may divide business men into two classes — those who take out of business and those who put in. The first class gets all it can for itself, in extreme situations leaving for others but a shell of emptiness. The second class, to which Mr. Cole belongs, is constantly adding to the usefulness, profit, and net worth of the business. Mr. Cole lives in and for the Harvard Co-operative Society. This society is his son and grandson in one. His spirit will live on through the years. But somebody will say, "this is a co-operative society and in co-operatives many men dominate." The answer is that, when co-operatives attain success, at least in the formative periods, one man really controls. Ability carves out an ample niche for itself.

As we have frequently seen, management turns on accounting and statistics. Mr. Cole began as expense manager and developed a budget system which has worked. In 1920 he raised the question of further changes in accounting methods. After attending a convention of controllers in the National Retail Dry Goods Association, he suggested that the "January inventory" be made upon a new basis. In 1921 the president and the manager conferred with representatives of the School of Business concerning the reclassification of expenses along the line of department-store practices. An accountant was secured through the School of Business to install the standard system of accounting sponsored by the National Retail Dry Goods Association. From this, it was expected, there would arise greater accuracy and better office work. Almost at once, reports were made to the Bureau of Business Research at the School of Business. Although these reports began in 1921, still they were not of high quality till 1926 and 1927. Thenceforth, the Society has been one of a group of department stores reporting a great variety of standardized data, the general averages of which are made known to all the participants. It must have become a source of satisfaction to Mr. Cole and to all the other officers to learn that the Co-operative compared very favorably at so many points. As we go through the comparable data of 1926–41, we find that the gross margin of profit of the Co-operative is much lower than in the average department store of its class and that variations from year to year do not run parallel; that the percentage of total expense is much lower for the Co-operative and also does not run parallel; that the rate of net profit is higher for the Co-operative and runs closely parallel with net profits in other comparable stores; and finally that the rate of losses of the Co-operative from bad debts is lower and runs roughly parallel.

In 1921 Harvard University became discontented with the employment of the Co-operative as a purchasing agent. The complaint was that prices were too high and that this arose through the alleged fact that the Co-operative "did not shop sufficiently." Next year Harvard appointed its own purchasing agent. As to whether the charge about inefficient buying is accurate or not, I have no way of forming an opinion.

At the present time, goods are purchased chiefly from the manufacturers. From the jobbers a few articles are still bought, such as small kitchen appliances, toys (perhaps 70 per cent of them), woolen cloth, and, very occasionally, books. Only a few commodities, the chief example being bed linens, are ever bought through commercial agents. In the history of the Co-operative, the whole subject of purchasing is, as far as records go, nearly a blank. I happen to know that in the history of other stores the situation is very similar.

Theft seems to be accelerated in the Society's history at one time, only to recede at a later date. In 1922 it was reckoned that 25 per cent of the shortages (underages) in the Main Store was "due to pilfering." It had been on the increase during the year to such an extent that a plan was developed to have the store shopped three times a year. Nothing is said in the records of the Society as to whether the pilfering was done by insiders or outsiders or both.

During 1922 the theater-ticket business showed a loss, a big loss. The business was closed. It had been full of difficulties, some of which pertained to the theatrical industry itself. One special embarrassment to the manager was to have an irate parent write in to inquire how it happened that his son's account had so much charged for theater tickets. In some cases, the explanation was that the boys had bought the tickets on credit and then raised ready cash by selling them to classmates.

In 1928 the manager sent circulars to residents of Arlington and Belmont and to students in the Medical School in order to popularize the Main Store. In December, 1929, when general trade was bad, "the suburban non-member trade" helped to save the day from the standpoint of sales. During this same year two Harvard professors, who were active in the administration of the Society, prepared a list of books useful for alumni. These were distributed to the extent of 13,000 copies. Few replies — 1,100 at the time of recording the fact — came in, practically none from Technology alumni. Whether the conclusion is that college graduates have had enough of education or buy their books elsewhere is not clear. At any rate, the Society has on several occasions done its best to promote adult education.

On the whole, I am impressed with the increasing cost of doing business in the Co-operative, as in other stores. This is exemplified chiefly by an increase in pay-roll costs which rose from 8.47 per cent of sales in 1921 to 13.45 per cent in 1940. Taxes also have skyrocketed, especially local taxes. Fortunately, the Society as a co-operative has been exempted from the federal corporation tax. The cost of hiring extra professional services has gone up, as has the cost of non-selling employees. Bad debts to the extent of an annual average of $3,082 were written off during the period of 11 years, 1930–40; but nearly all of these debts were later recovered. The difference between bad debts written off and those recovered during the 6

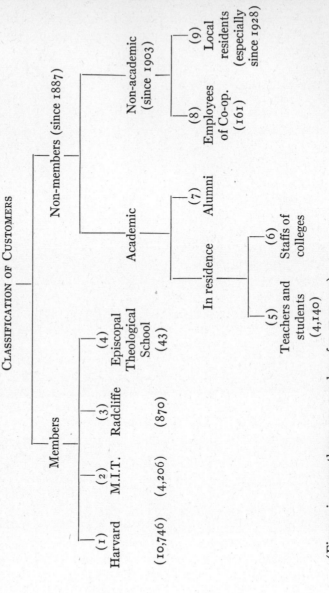

CLASSIFICATION OF CUSTOMERS

Members

(1) Harvard (10,746)
(2) M.I.T. (4,206)
(3) Radcliffe (870)
(4) Episcopal Theological School (43)

Non-members (since 1887)

Academic

In residence
(5) Teachers and students (4,140)
(6) Staffs of colleges

(7) Alumni

Non-academic (since 1903)
(8) Employees of Co-op. (161)
(9) Local residents (especially since 1928)

(Figures in parentheses are numbers for 1941–42.)

years 1936–41 was $644, annual average. But there is a clerical and interest cost involved in these delayed payments that the Co-operative should not have to bear. There seems to be no pronounced trend in bad debts either up or down. Fortunately, there were no great increases in certain other costs, such as advertising, interest, or real estate.

The story of the Society's use of publicity can be written in detail, at least in so far as it deals with advertising. From the first, the Society has advertised in the college papers. Ordinarily it was stock goods that were listed for sale — books, pens, sport goods, furnishings, and so on. In 1901 the *Diary of a Freshman* was listed and at about the same time the fountain pens of the first superintendent — A. A. Waterman. Bargains are occasionally found in the college-paper advertisements; for example, in 1896 "White duck trousers at less than cost," in 1903 the clearance of furniture at 28 Church Street, and the January sales — in 1905 a reduction sale and in 1906 a markdown sale. An institutional advertisement in the *Harvard Lampoon* in 1921 said that "the savings which the Coop makes for its members is the Co-operative's only justification for existence." Perhaps "only" should be "chief."

We have statistics that are reliable from 1926 to the present. The highest cost of publicity in a single year was in 1940–41, when $21,757 were spent. The lowest since 1926 was $14,173 in 1932–33. While publicity was 1.55 per cent of net sales in the period 1926–40, advertising alone was 1.13 per cent in 1929–40. In recent years, we note a decline in advertising in college newspapers and a rise in the use of non-college or suburban newspapers and in advertising by mail. In general, however, the Harvard Co-operative spends very much less for publicity and advertising than do other comparable department stores.

Into the little world of a single store there began to enter with the N.R.A. in 1933 a new business régime, namely, national capitalism, which we call the New Deal. On September 15, 1933, the president of the Co-operative asked the manager to report on the Society's relation to the N.R.A. This was official recognition that something new had been born.

Fortunately, in October, 1933, an order was issued over President Roosevelt's signature that co-operatives are not to be prohibited from paying "patronage dividends," if they are "paid out of actual earnings — and are not paid at the time when such member makes a purchase." In other words, patronage dividends are not unfair discounts. Even though the N.R.A. was itself short-lived, still the general growing control from Washington was to continue. There were maximum hours of work and a minimum wage. All employees go under the federal Social Security pension scheme. All this involves more work for the manager and less for the policy-formulators of the Society.

In 1935 the increasing competition at Harvard Square was becoming apparent; and there was even talk of Macy's opening up a branch. The manager faced all this squarely, seeing in it a challenge to his mettle. The chief weapon open to him was the reduction of prices. The subject of prices was also becoming a ramified problem under the New Deal. Various price maintenance laws were passed. Some firms insisted that the Society should pay no dividends on their particular wares, for such dividends were by way of unjustifiable rebates. Here was a challenge to the very foundation of the Society's business, as well as to the legal counsel, Professor Scott. No judicial interpretation justified such an extreme attitude and so, for the time being, the issue was dormant. But such situations bring the manager and the legal counsel into frequent conference.

During the decade 1920–30 there was a gradual change in the system of using affiliated stores for the purpose of buying goods not carried by the Co-operative. Originally, the Co-operative's members went to any of the stores named in the Co-operative's printed list, purchased the goods they wished, and then, on showing their Co-operative membership tickets, received a discount for cash payment. During the decade of the 1920's, however, the change in this system was accelerated from a cash purchase basis to an order basis. Then, increasingly, the Co-operative members were required to get an order from the Co-operative which they presented on purchasing goods. The goods purchased were then billed to the Co-operative and delivered to the member's address. This change in the mode of purchase reflected a change in the list of affiliated stores. There had been a tendency for retailers to give up special arrangements with the Co-operative. Wholesalers and wholesale-retailers, however, who were already selling to the Co-operative directly, no matter in how small amounts, were willing to sell to the Co-operative's members on order. Thus, this constituted a transaction at the wholesale level and could be less challenged on the ground of business ethics. In form, the Co-operative purchased at wholesale rates and the members received a dividend. Thus, for discount there has been substituted a dividend — a more round-about way to the same end.

The Society seems to have sold its horse and delivery wagons in 1920 and to have purchased automobiles. In 1922 it refused to go into the grocery, real-estate, and house-and-room rental business. In 1933 it refused to take advantage of the dying agonies of prohibition and add to its lines the items of wines and liquors. Next year it was announced that some of the officials of the Yale Co-operative Society would visit the Main Store. Indeed, I have been told that the manager of the Yale Co-operative knows the Harvard Co-operative very well.

How a store weathers a business crisis is always a matter of interest. On September 20, 1929, Mr. Cole reported that, although the inventory was large, "there is nothing to worry about." Within two months he had "plans for curtailing orders for certain divisions because of the business outlook." During the dark years of the depression, the Society did rather well. Even before the clouds had lifted, the manager was ready to develop new business. In February, 1932, he was introducing electrical appliances. Just after the bank holiday in March, 1933, a new optical department was opened. In the same year a woman's hosiery department was embarked upon, which has proved a great success, though only high-class firsts, no high-class seconds, are sold. During the winter of 1933–34 a ski department was established to meet a new fad in sports. If the fad survives the War, the Society will be lucky, for it has an ample supply of skis on hand.

Many things were added, some few were lost. In 1934 it was necessary to abandon the sale of coal, oil, and wood under the N.R.A. But later, a contract was arranged for the purchase by members of gas and oil and service in washing and polishing cars.

War has again made threatening grimaces at the Co-operative. The Spanish-American War it hardly noted. The first World War it adjusted itself to very nicely. That was largely a matter of facing economic reality in a world of price economics. Now prices are kept down and costs up. The business man is supposed to struggle between the upper and the nether millstones. In 1940 members protested against the sale of Japanese and German goods. In 1941 the manager reported that he was "covering the needs of various departments because of the uncertainty" of future supplies. Some employees had been drafted and others had gone into war industry. Bonuses had to be provided to meet the increasing cost of living. Anxiety and extra work (of the manager and others working long over-time) arose from such principal controls from Washington as the following in 1941–42:

(a) Cutting down on deliveries in order to save rubber tires.
(b) Freezing of the sale of certain articles, notably typewriters and refrigerators.
(c) Ceiling on prices.
(d) Curtailment of credit.

To make the picture more precarious, it has been announced that control of inventory is to come next. And so the manager must anxiously scan the morning paper to learn what his main job is to be next.

What a lot of things there are to look out for! A summary of the work of the manager would be to control stock and the prices at which goods are sold and to keep costs of all kinds at a minimum, so that there will be a net profit. The manager is charged with these duties and acquits himself well. After he creates the profits, however, there are still problems to be dealt with, as we shall see in the next section.

§10. President Henry S. Thompson: financial strength. No one has watched the Co-operative grow for so long a time as Mr. Henry S. Thompson. In fact, since 1910 Mr. Thompson has been intimately concerned with the Society. Since 1922 he has been president.

Like Kip and Waterman, Mr. Thompson came from the Middle West. Born in Senecaville, Ohio, on October 5, 1871, Mr. Thompson was graduated from the Ohio High School at Barnesville in 1891. During 1892–93 he was employed by a quartz concern in Indiana. After spending two years at DePauw University, he went to Harvard where he was graduated in 1899. Then he was employed by the Harvard Union till 1901. For several years he was concurrently graduate treasurer of athletics, secretary of appointments, and treasurer of the Harvard Union. In all these offices he had come to know Harvard exceedingly well and to be highly regarded by the University officials.

Mr. Thompson has been closely associated with outside business since 1907. Until 1912 he was associated with Philip Cabot and others in developing electric properties in the Connecticut Valley. He was a general partner in White, Weld and Company, 1912–16. Then he was financial secretary of the Harvard Medical School. During 1923–27 he was with the investment bankers, Coffin and Burr; during 1927–32 with the Franklin Management Corporation, investment counsellors; during 1932–35 with the Harvard Economic Society under Professor C. J. Bullock; and since 1935 he has been associated with H. C. Wainwright and Company. Thus we see that the central emphasis of Mr. Thompson's work has been financial.

These facts have been presented to indicate the experience and background that Mr. Thompson has had for his work as head of the Co-operative. Add to all this a fine personality, a decent respect for other men and their opinions, and the ability to act as a catalyst in any business group, and we have a combination that the Co-operative Society can use to great profit. Always, Mr. Thompson has rendered invaluable service by being fair to both customers and employees. And we must not forget the affection and loyalty that he has for Harvard institutions, an affection that makes him sacrifice self for service.

As president, Mr. Thompson has not merely presided over the board of directors; he has shared with the manager and others the burden of getting things done and of doing things. He has given the manager helpful support and has encouraged initiative. He has the interests of the student members of the Society constantly in mind. He has a fine record for attendance at the board meetings. And, of course, he has regarded matters of long-time finance and financial policy as his particular responsibility. In 1925 the Society authorized the issue of $90,000 worth of debenture bonds to run not over 10 years at 6 per cent interest. Of this amount, $50,000 were for paying off the second mortgage on the new building and $40,000 were to pay off the bank loans. These were gold bonds; and those that were actually sold were marketed at par. By 1929 these bonds had been wholly redeemed. And by 1934 the mortgage, which had stood at $292,500 in 1926, was wholly paid off. Doubtless Mr. Thompson took great satisfaction in this record.

To any member of the Society who is interested in finance, there could hardly be any more pleasant task than to study the Treasurer's Reports during the presidency of Mr. Thompson. The real estate, equipment, and merchandise came to be held without any debt. The surplus of the Society grew to handsome proportions. Reserves were held against all anticipated contingencies. And the current assets were in fine shape. The current assets (cash and securities) may be summarized as follows:

Period	No. of Years	Annual Average
1906–19	13	$ 6,119.40
1919–42	23	129,804.05

Of course, someone may say that there is too much cash (earning a very low rate of interest) for the needs of the store, but the evidence of the near future is not all in. And someone else

HENRY S. THOMPSON, PRESIDENT SINCE 1922

may say that this fine financial showing was made possible by the prosperity of the American people as reflected in Cambridge and by the efficient management of the manager who, through thick and thin, has been able to produce a net profit.

But here is a capital point. Amid all the pressure — slight enough perhaps — to pay out more net profit in the form of dividends, the president has stood firm for the addition of a sizable amount of the profit to surplus. He is pleased with the possibility of high dividends but does not like to see the rate of dividend go higher than can be maintained through the years. When we think of the fact that the whole period beginning in 1920 has shown a downward trend in prices and profits, we must admit that the showing of the Co-operative has been excellent.

In the financial work of the Society, Mr. Thompson's responsibilities have been shared by all the officers as well as by the directors. Since 1940 the new treasurer, Mr. Horace S. Ford, for 21 years previously a director of the Society, has raised expectations of unusually efficient work in an office that had been characterized by altogether too much routine. Mr. Ford, who as a young man had been prevented from entering Harvard College by the death of his father, served a splendid apprenticeship in the Old Colony Trust Company, from which he went to the Massachusetts Institute of Technology as bursar in 1913. After 21 years of this service, he became treasurer of the Institute on a full-time basis. He has been sought after as director by various business concerns. It has been the good fortune of the Society to be able to enlist the part-time service of such an official — who combines ability, experience, geniality, and effective co-operation. Since becoming treasurer of the Society, he has sponsored a change in the auditing of the Society's accounts. Instead of having the treasurer select the auditor to examine the accounts, the new arrangement, proposed in 1940, is to have a committee of the board of directors select an auditor who reports on both the treasurer's and the manager's accounts. In so far as this involves the use of an auditing committee as intermediary, it is a return to the earliest practices of the Society.

Moreover, he has also sponsored an inventory of buildings, equipment, and merchandise which may become of great value in tax situations in the future.

In a general way, we can see three overlapping stages in the history of the Harvard Co-operative Society. The first is the régime of petty capitalism from 1882 onward to about 1903. Then came the régime of industrial capitalism which began in the 1890's and was established by 1903. The stage that follows industrial capitalism is normally financial capitalism or the control of business by investment bankers — a system much condemned in America and, as we shall probably learn some day, unjustly condemned. The alternative to this kind of régime is financial-industrial capitalism, of which Mr. Thompson, a financial industrialist, has been the protagonist. In financial-industrial capitalism, the work of the outside financial capitalist (ordinarily on Wall Street, or State Street) is done by some official on the inside (Mr. Thompson in the Co-operative), someone with an eye to long-time policies, ample reserves, strong cash position, and generally even tenor of performance. Examples of financial-industrial capitalism are Swift and Company, the Ford Motor Company, R. H. Macy and Company, and the Harvard Co-operative Society.

BUSINESS RÉGIMES EXEMPLIFIED BY THE SOCIETY'S GROWTH

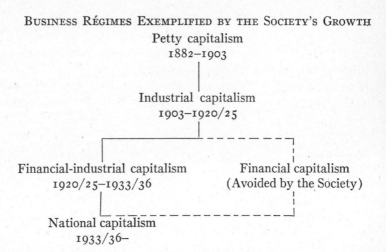

Petty capitalism
1882–1903

Industrial capitalism
1903–1920/25

Financial-industrial capitalism   Financial capitalism
1920/25–1933/36   (Avoided by the Society)

National capitalism
1933/36–

In financial-industrial capitalism the Society has developed managerial efficiency, it has enunciated and followed out a long-time financial policy, and it has secured independence of commercial banks and avoided the control of investment bankers. Indeed, the Harvard Co-operative Society has never gone to Wall Street. Its dealings have been with local commercial banks, such as the Harvard Trust Company and particularly the Cambridge Trust Company, and with the Old Colony Trust Company of Boston only for some intermediate financing.

Just as financial capitalism began to show its head slightly above the ground under the industrial-capitalist régime of President Munro, so has national capitalism already begun to develop during the régime of President Thompson. If we wish to project our imagination into the future of the Society, we should think along the line of influences from Washington. On the surface of the record, Mr. Thompson's main contributions may be regarded as completed by 1934–36, when the Society was out of debt and in a strong cash position, whilst the New Deal stream of influence began in 1933.

§11. Problems ahead of the Society. An historian is supposed to stick to the past. He is expected to have a lively feeling for what is dead. But to me history is a waste of time if not useful. Moreover, I see no line between the past, present, and future. By imaginative projection the past slips over the present into the future. Indeed, without this anticipation, no real understanding of the recent past is possible. But in any effort to envisage the future, through a study of the past, we need not be dogmatic and we cannot be sure. I submit nine points for consideration.

First, the maturity and stability attained by the Society may spell stagnation. In history, when an institution or firm has reached a certain perfection and has solved its chief problems, then it is in danger of going down hill. Without serious challenges, effort is absent or becomes routine. To be sure, there are problems in plenty on the horizon, and several that are now to be specifically mentioned; and for these we should be thankful if they do not become crushing.

Second, the excellence of the policy since 1903 of emphasizing the profitable part of the available business may be dangerous, if too long followed. I think of this as but a phase, some day to be discontinued. Already there have been modifications of the policy. Certainly it has been proper and effective in building up strength. At this point in the Society's history, attention may well be given to more service, even if less profitable. This might be developed particularly in handling less expensive but still serviceable lines, required by persons and families of low income or by anyone for some purposes. Of course, the gross profit might be less and the expense of handling might be more per dollar of value, and therefore the net profit to the Society might be less. There is a possibility, however, that this lower profit could be countered by a sufficient increase in volume, necessitating even the use of the two topmost stories of the main building. I do not expect that this would cut in upon the trade of small stores at Harvard Square but would be somewhat at the expense of Boston stores.

Third, I have no doubt that the manager, if asked, would have put the problem of competition first. He has had to wrestle with chain specialty stores, chain novelty stores, and, about one mile away, a chain department store which is also a mail-order house. It was not so difficult for the Co-operative to compete with little unit stores of the petty capitalist variety, while it grew on into industrial and financial-industrial capitalism. But, when it has to compete with such firms as Woolworth and Sears Roebuck, the situation is different. And, so long as the Co-operative puts emphasis on the profitable part of business, there will be opportunities for an increasing number of competitors. Thus, we come back to our second problem. The whole future of retailing (including fair trade laws) is involved at this point.

Fourth, there is the increase in the cost of doing business. This is all but universal, but it may grow to such proportions as to threaten the fat dividends now being paid. If the dividend should go down from 12 to 10 to 8 to 6 to 4 per cent, there would be a considerable loss in membership and in sales. And, if this trend should continue at a time when the student body was diminishing, as may well happen in a country where there is a feeling that much collegiate instruction is a waste of time as at present organized, then the result could be disastrous.

Fifth, there lies some danger in the increase in sales that are not dividend-bearing (39 per cent of the total in 1907–08). At present, there are three categories of such sales: (a) all sales under 25 cents — a mere device to save in the cost of book-keeping, (b) sales charged but not followed by prompt payment, and (c) purchases made by non-members. A small number of such sales would still leave the Society co-operative, but a large number might open the question of exemption from the federal corporation income tax. The most recent figures are gratifying. They show that for 1941–42 the percentage of non-dividend bearing sales was as follows: Main Store 28, School of Business Branch 19, and Technology Store 30.

Sixth, there is the continuing problem of the affiliated stores. Originally, the chance to pool the buying resources of students and instructors was important. Today it exists largely as an irritant. Some stores have abandoned the plan. In most cases there is nothing much for the dealer in giving what amounts to a discount to a Co-operative ticket-holder. Nominally, the reward to the dealer may be for cash payment from the Society, but why not give the favor to the firm's regular customers? Better business practice tends to get away from this sort of procedure.

Seventh, the Society still has a good deal of slack in its potential market that might be taken up. The record of the increase in the percentage of membership among students and teachers eligible to membership is very creditable, as figures in Appendix 8, below, show. But, until this year, there has been little progress in the last decade. The problem has been how to induce about 5,000 eligibles to join the Society. Certainly, this is not to be done on the ground of loyalty to colleges, for the Co-operative is almost wholly on a business basis. It could be done by continuing the old methods of offering more goods, some at lower prices, and more services. True, all this is easier

(They are all ticket-holders, all participating members, all investing customers, and all possess the right to share in dividends and to purchase from affiliated tradesmen.)

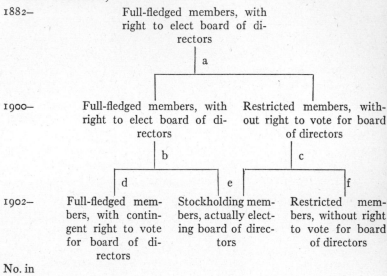

1882—
Full-fledged members, with right to elect board of directors

a

1900—
Full-fledged members, with right to elect board of directors

b

Restricted members, without right to vote for board of directors

c

1902—

d
Full-fledged members, with contingent right to vote for board of directors

e
Stockholding members, actually electing board of directors

f
Restricted members, without right to vote for board of directors

No. in
1942   7,213   10   8,642

Note: (a) Members were not differentiated in respect to voting till 1900.
     (b) Actual officers and students at Harvard University and Radcliffe College.
     (c) Alumni and unclassified of Harvard and members connected with Radcliffe and the Episcopal Theological School.
     (d) This group might exercise their alternative and dormant right to elect the board of directors. They are the actual or present officers and students of Harvard University.
     (e) The stockholders or trustees meet at least twice a year and actually nominate and elect the board of directors. Probably there is no requirement that they be members but in practice they are.
     (f) These are the same as (c) except that, beginning in 1902, members from Radcliffe were added and, in 1916, members from Technology. The two groups (d) and (f) possess rights in common of voting on at least five constitutional occasions, any or all of which may become actual. The members in (d) and certain ones in (f) (Harvard and Technology) share the right to hold certain offices.

said than done, but it may become a means out of a difficult situation during such hard times as may follow a great war.

Eighth, making the Society co-operative in administration is still a problem and will remain so, just as long as students (ever so few) at Harvard and Technology so regard it. In these days of democratic inefficiency, it is no argument to say "but we have an efficient oligarchy, why disturb it?" (Our colleges, hospitals, business units, and homes are also petty oligarchies calmly prospering in a seething democracy.) Perhaps we might begin by considering the following: (a) Transfer the three Harvard undergraduate directorships to the (board of) stockholders, each to hold for three years. I should not fear this dilution, and it would have the effect of giving representation to the many where it should be — in the ranks of the stockholders. (b) Put into the places of the three undergraduate directors two students from the School of Business and one from the Law School. These men are equipped by knowledge and interest to be useful as directors. (c) Encourage the ticket-holders to elect a small advisory council which would sit once a year with the (board of) stockholders and once a year with the board of directors. Let these councillors be paid a fee for each of these sessions. Encourage them to be active in giving advice. Creating such a council would mean the implementing of existing machinery even more than the creation of new mechanism. Doing all this would require the constant attention of an official or a director of the Society, but it would be more than an empty gesture. Moreover, it is good policy and procedure to get ideas from customers and clients. In case of an emergency, such a council might save the day for the Society.

Ninth, the constitution is complicated and needs revision. Perhaps the over-amended documents could be put into one, and the present duality of corporation and unincorporated association abolished. At present, probably not even the officers understand the constitution at all points. This complexity deters the interest of anyone who approaches the Society either from the standpoint of participation in its affairs or from the standpoint of understanding its working.

At this point we need to stop to consider just what the constitution of the Harvard Co-operative Society really is. Technically, according to the custom of the Society, the constitution is a set of nine clauses enacted or re-enacted in 1900. But, in reality, this is the constitution of the old unlimited partnership that was ceremoniously interred in January, 1903. In no real sense is this the constitution of the living Society of today, any more than the by-laws of 1900 are the by-laws of the present organization. In truth, the constitution of the Society is found in the by-laws which went into effect in 1903 and which have been revised from time to time by the (board of) stockholders. This constitution, however, cannot be interpreted or enforced without disinterring the constitution of 1900. Moreover, it is complicated, badly arranged, and in places obscure. It was not made so by design but by circumstances that were met just as they arose. These circumstances are as follows: the need for a new administrative mechanism in 1902, the requirements (from 1903 onward) of a corporation formed under the laws of Massachusetts, and the shifting conditions of day-to-day growth. And so, I should say, the constitution that needs revision is the living constitution of 1903 and following years ("by-laws"), taken in conjunction with the buried constitution of 1900.

Of course, I know the arguments against proposals for change. Why not let good enough alone? A firm as prosperous as the Co-operative needs no jacking up. But my point is that every firm needs progressive change all the time and needs it most when it least thinks so. I hope that all this does not make me a Progressive.

CHAPTER VI

SERVICES — PAST AND PRESENT

§1. Influence on other college co-operatives. The Harvard Co-operative Society has had the heavy responsibility through the years of being a kind of paradigm of college co-operatives. Known as the earliest, it has been thought the wisest. In other words, like Harvard University it has suffered from the halo of age — a strength and a weakness. The records prove how one institution after another, from at least 1884, has written in, or sent an emissary, to find out how the Harvard Co-operative Society is organized and administered. As we have seen, during one year, 1884–85, it was such faith abroad, which surpassed local confidence, that really saved the Harvard Co-operative. If others thought it good, there must be something in it. If others think that we know how to administer a co-operative, we must measure up to our reputation. This was the case for only that one hectic year, but it was a fundamental factor at that time.

Possibly the following graph is sufficiently accurate and suggestive to be considered.

POSSIBLE GENESIS OF COLLEGE CO-OPERATIVES

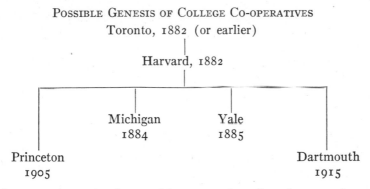

Toronto, 1882 (or earlier)

Harvard, 1882

Michigan 1884   Yale 1885

Princeton 1905   Dartmouth 1915

I do not mean to imply anything more than that the experiences of the older institutions were considered by the college groups planning a co-operative of their own. Certainly, if the Harvard group of February, 1882, actually knew about the situation at Toronto, as it did by the following April, it did not follow the example closely. Also, it should be noted that the early efforts at Michigan and Dartmouth came to grief.

In analyzing the various influences that have moulded college co-operatives in America, I should put down the following: the pressing local college need, the general co-operative movement, the local variations as worked out by farmers and laborers, and a desire to learn from Harvard's experiences without imitating Harvard. This does not seem to leave much room for service on the part of the Harvard Co-operative; but an examination of college co-operatives does actually disclose some diffusion of Harvard policies. I shall leave to others the disclosure of copying or adopting, except to say that the University of Michigan (earliest efforts), Yale, Princeton, and Cornell seem to be examples of some borrowing.

On the whole, I am more impressed with the variations of co-operatives in American colleges than with the uniformity and borrowing. In other words, effusion as well as diffusion has played its part. This will be illustrated by a rough survey of the situation of co-operatives in American colleges, based upon over 200 inquiries, which indicates a number of different categories, eight of which are here set down.

First, some colleges have no co-operatives of any kind and are proud of the fact. In some cases the size of the college is too small to support a co-operative, and the pride arises after this fact has been recognized. In other cases, there are college-owned bookstores or community co-operatives which sell stationery as well as textbooks and obviate the need for a college co-operative.

Second, many colleges have no co-operatives of any kind but are not proud of the fact. Many colleges have tried but failed. Others have just never got around to it. In the case of one Virginia college, the local explanation is summed up in two lines:

> "Ole Virginia never tire
> 'Cause she go so slo'."

Third, a few colleges have co-operatives in name only. Examples are Dartmouth College at present and the University of Minnesota.

Fourth, many colleges and universities have co-operatives in credit, rooming, eating, cleaning and pressing, and so on. At times, the credit is for teachers and other employees. In general, State universities exemplify this category.

Fifth, some colleges and universities have a variety of co-operatives, including a buying society. The instructors at the University of Louisiana have organized a buying pool for their own benefit.

Sixth, some institutions have various kinds of co-operatives including a mere bookstore administered by the members.

Seventh, there is at least one college co-operative (at Stanford) that is faculty controlled (like Harvard's) but gives to both students and members of the faculty a rebate on purchases. It is a bookstore, however, not a department store. At the University of Texas the faculty has a majority of representatives on the board of directors, the students a slight minority.

Eighth, a few, such as Harvard, Yale, Princeton, and Cornell, have co-operatives of various kinds including, or perhaps specially, a general or department store.

We might classify college co-operatives according to the use to which they put their net profits. One group of co-operatives pays out all its net profits to some kind of charity or to support a service, just as though paying dividends to individuals was unchristian. Some co-operatives, notably those in Jesuit colleges, devote their earnings to college organizations, such as debating societies. The Bryn Mawr co-operative uses its profits to support scholarships. A second class pays part of its earnings to charity and a part to members. The State College of Washington pays 85 per cent to members as dividends and 15 per cent for the purpose of education in co-operation. The third class is made up of those which pay all their dividends to members but also retain a part of net profits to build up a surplus for future years and for fresh, unforeseeable purposes. The

Harvard Co-operative Society belongs to this class and has attained notable success along the lines of this policy.

A comparison of the situations in several large co-operative societies is seen in the table on page 129.

There is much that is suggestive in the table, but further study would be required before any conclusions could be drawn. I wonder whether Eastern college co-operatives tend to build up a surplus, whilst the Western do not emphasize this aspect so much as low prices. I wonder whether 10 per cent is about the normal present rate of dividends where dividends are paid. I wonder whether about half the co-operatives are on a membership-fee basis, whilst the other half are not.

It is very probable that the Harvard Co-operative Society has really had some influence on other co-operatives over the years; but clearly the dominant factor is the local consumptive need and the local attitude to business. I wonder whether any other co-operative has followed the Harvard Co-operative in devising legalistic complexities. If the Harvard Co-operative Society's constitution were made more simple and more democratic, the influence would grow. But, then, I assume that the Harvard Co-operative was not designed as a democratic model: it was originally designed, and is still kept keyed, to serve local current needs. Long may this purpose reign!

There has been one place where the Harvard Co-operative Society has hardly been a follower, to say nothing of leadership. I refer to the work of the National Committee on Student Co-operatives and the National Association of College Stores. There seem to be few persons in the Harvard Co-operative Society interested in the co-operative movement as such. Indeed, the history of the Society since 1903 rather points to success in spite of, or because of a lack of sympathy with, the co-operative movement as generally propagated. One notable example of this has been the lack of any emphasis upon education in co-operation. The Harvard emphasis has been upon private business, notably in its School of Business; and the success of the Harvard Co-operative has been attained largely because it has followed the best traditions of private business. I had thought

A Comparison of Six College Co-operatives showing Condition in 1940-41

Univ.	Date est'd	Date incorp.	No. of Members	An. Vol. of Sales	Dividend[a] %	Surplus or Gen. Res. $	Ownership of Building
Harvard	1882	1903	14,345	1,420,000	12 / 10	843,634	Yes
Yale	1885	1893	4,215	509,000	11 / 8½	190,000	No
Wisconsin	1892 / 1914	Corp. Trust[e]	59,670[b]	170,000	10	85,427[c]	No[d]
Cornell	1895	1905	Open[f]	287,709	10	124,622	No[g]
Texas	1896	1906	[12,300][h]	180,858	0[i]	3,304	Yes
Princeton	1905	1905	3,503	465,275	10	187,045	No

a When two rates of dividends are given, the first is for cash sales and the second is for charge sales.
b Life memberships; no charge for membership.
c Net worth.
d Holds lease of building from the University of Wisconsin with an equity therein.
e A common law trust.
f No longer any membership requirement.
g Owns a warehouse (land and building) worth about $19,000.
h Those students and faculty members who are in residence.
i Dividends discontinued in favor of lower prices.

that this book might be entitled "Twenty Years of Co-operation and Forty Years of Success."

§2. Goods and services abandoned or lost. It is a wise retailer who abandons lines that are not profitable. Certainly this has been the policy of the Society from at least 1903 onward. The Medical School Branch was sold in that year and with it went the business in medical books and supplies. As we have seen, the handling of Law School books was lost in 1905 because of the difficulty in making a profit. Of course, one wonders whether the losses might not have been made up by the purchase of other articles by Law School students. It should be noted, however, that in recent years this business in Law School books has been regained. In the Society's Main Store there is commonly no department that does not pay for itself. (But in 1941–42 both the tailoring and textbook departments actually showed deficits.) Paints and hardware were abandoned after a period of considerable sales. Somehow the Society never learned how to handle these commodities profitably — especially at a time of great rivalry in three small local hardware stores, one large chain novelty store carrying a line of hardware, and a chain department store one mile away with a large assortment of hardware and particularly of paints at reasonable prices. And so the paints and hardware have been sold off gradually.

We have observed that the mail-order business in stationery and particularly in books was cultivated and then abandoned. Theater tickets were long sold at the Harvard Square Branch, but finally losses became too heavy to justify the continuance of the service. A leased department — flowers — was tried but abandoned, probably because it took up too much space. A travel bureau was set up but got too little business. The shoe-mending business, once of fair size, has been abandoned but when and under what circumstances I have not noted.

The Co-operative lost the purchasing of goods for Harvard University because the prices were considered by the University to be too high. Other services and goods have been abandoned because of the change in circumstances. Once a brisk trade was done in the second-hand commission business, not only in text-books but in furniture. Indeed, it was one of the main objects of the Society at first to perform these services. Although the second-hand book business remains, the furniture business has been lost.

The coal and wood business was lost when snuffed out by the N.R.A.; it was never taken up again. Perhaps the activity of the Purchasing Department of Harvard University along these lines is in part the explanation of the Society's not re-entering the business. Of course, the Society never owned coal or wood yards; it merely took orders which were filled by regular dealers at reduced prices. During the present year, circumstances have forced the Society to discontinue the contract-pressing business. This was because of the difficulty of getting tires for the trucks; and contract pressing was largely a matter of calling (and calling again) for clothes and then delivering on the first or second effort. The pressing of clothes brought in by the members, however, has not been abandoned.

§3. Special services — paid for and free. The two outstanding services paid for are the pressing of clothes and the laundering of linen. The former has already been considered. The laundry business is a service to those whose linen is regularly washed and ironed and also to the students who get the contracts for the work. The rivalry in this business is considerable. Complaints are common as in all laundry work. The Co-operative formerly let the contract to Cambridge firms but always had difficulty in getting prompt delivery. Now the contract is awarded to a firm in another town and with great satisfaction. This laundry service is a large item in the Co-operative's total business, being exceeded at the Main Store by only the stationery, men's furnishing, book, ready-to-wear, and house furnishing departments. In no sense can this service be regarded as exclusive: there are other and competing laundry services on every hand.

Providing caps and gowns on the occasion of commencement exercises and of special academic celebrations is also a great service, since neither professor nor student regularly uses such archaic garb. The staff likes to remember the amusing stories about misfitting gowns just as the victims like to forget the circumstance. But normally all goes as smoothly as the wearing of strange feathers will permit.

The free services are important to the members for what they get directly and to the Society for what it gets indirectly — good will. The outstanding example is the cashing of checks, which grew up in the early years of the Society's history. A member on presenting his ticket, and, if a student, also his bursar's card, can have a check (not over $100) cashed to his great convenience, particularly in case he has no account in the adjoining banks or in case the banks are closed. In February, 1941, the newspapers reported a loss of $95 from a bad check cashed by the Society. This was unusual. The annual loss is only about $200 out of over $2,000,000 worth of checks cashed each year. Indeed, in the bank crash of 1933 the Society lost only $270 from bad checks. I believe that the Yale Co-operative charges 10 cents for each check cashed. A similar plan has been proposed for the Harvard Co-operative, but the decision has been that this service is worth what it costs: it builds up good friends for the Society. Indeed, it would be interesting to know how many students actually pay their dollar in September solely for the enjoyment of this advantage. To be sure, they may buy more or less merchandise later on, and that is the logic of the plan.

The Society maintains a service for the transfer of luggage by a Boston transfer company. This often obviates a trip over-town or at least a telephone call. The members of the Society also have the privilege of asking one of the two or three notaries public in the Main Store to attest official documents with their seal and without charge. In these days of growing officialdom this is of real assistance.

On the occasion of special events the Society is ready to assist its members, the colleges that support it, and the community. Moderate expenses for such purposes are cheerfully borne.

BOOK DEPARTMENT, MAIN STORE, 1942

§4. Service through the sale of goods. It would be tedious to rehearse the story of the building-up of departments of goods. At the present time the board of directors receives and examines monthly figures from 17 departments, including those for gasoline sold to members by a neighboring service station. Missing among the departments in the Main Store are jewelry, silverware, women's wear, groceries, and wines and liquors.

I think that it is not an exaggeration to say that the book department and the book-ordering service are worthy adjuncts to the educational institutions served. I have in mind the handling of general books even more than the trade in textbooks. It is a curious fact that Americans are not a book-reading people. When they have become so, the historian will record the contribution of the Harvard Co-operative.

Accurate, discriminating, and proud of attainment as are the members of the Harvard Co-operative, they do have difficulty when ordering books from memory. Mrs. Knox of the book department has given me a list of some titles asked for in recent years.

Correct Titles	Titles asked for by Customers
Studs Lonigan	Stud in Love Again
The Citadel	The City Dump
Gone with the Wind	Away with the Breeze
How Odd of God	Oh God, how could You do it?
Music, History, and Ideas	Art, Painting, and Things
Scaramouche	Scarlet Mouse
Mortal Storm	Moral Wrong
Brothers Karamazov	Brothers Carry Me Off (Radcliffe)
War and Peace	Warren Peace
Journey of Tapiola	Tale of Tapioca
The Snow Goose	The White Swan
The Sun is My Undoing	My Son is My Undoing

It often happens that a member wants not only a book but something else not kept in stock. Here the Society's clerks are ready to advise and to assist in the purchase of almost any commodity. Furniture or other goods may be bought in this way, from descriptions secured from catalogues or elsewhere. To the lazy shopper or to the busy person this is a great boon.

Of all the services performed by the Co-operative the sale of goods is, of course, the greatest. Indeed, this is one of the greatest social services known to man and in no sense peculiar to the Co-operative. We rarely stop to consider the planning and the work involved in anticipating our wishes, selecting the goods, stocking them, and keeping the supply varied and up to date. It happens that we have figures for the sale of goods and services by the Society from March, 1882, to June, 1942. Unless I have added wrongly, the total is $34,778,938.33. Thus, the annual average for 60 years is $579,648.97.

Added to this volume of sales is the business done through the Society in the affiliated stores. Once the volume was considerable, now it seems to be dwindling fast. There are no statistics. In recent years the annual volume has been only about $5,000; however, the annual sale of gas, oil, and service to members by a neighboring dealer, under special arrangement, has been over eight times this amount.

§5. Prices and dividends. It would be heroic to attempt to discover how much the Society has saved its members and others by reducing prices at Harvard Square. For many years, that was its chief service. Then came a time when the prices of the Society's goods were on a par with those at the Square. If there was henceforth any reduction, it was casual or forced by the Society's competitors. Henceforth, the price advantage to the member arose exclusively through dividends. And yet, before the incoming of the chain stores, perhaps the whole Harvard Square price level would have gone back to super-Boston heights as before the establishment of the Society, if the Society should have been discontinued.

Although the savings through the reduction in prices cannot be reckoned, we can determine the dividends. During the whole period of its history (60 years) the Society has paid to its members $2,055,118.35, or an annual average of $34,251.97. Good accounting practice puts these payments down as "dividends;"

the lore of co-operation sometimes regards them as "patronage refunds," or "savings" on competitive prices. Whatever the name, they are the rewards of good policy-formulation and good management, plus a heavy dose of charitable donation on the part of a few individuals, plus some advantage from location or clientèle.

From another standpoint we may tentatively regard the members or ticket-holders as investing capitalists. Certainly no one would deny that the original group in 1882 were such. From this standpoint, in a period of 60 years, the investing capitalists, putting in $345,897.50 as dues, received back $2,055,118.35 as dividends, that is, at the rate of 595 per cent. For the year 1941–42 the rate has been 839 per cent. But do not hurry to invest on these terms alone. There is one thing that the member has had to do, after he has put down his dollar and before he could get back $5.95 or $8.39: he has had to buy a certain amount of goods or services. And thus we see that we should speak of the "investing customer" rather than just the "investing capitalist." Therein lies the catch from the standpoint of one having capital to invest.

And, finally, there is the service of the Society as such — a vital going organization of men and women performing the full functions of buying, storing, and selling goods, paying taxes, employing many individuals, and belonging to various trade associations that play a part in our general life. It is of such units that our business régime is made up and it is upon such units that in times of stress, as in times of equilibrium, we have to depend. The Harvard Co-operative Society, like any such business, is the resultant of many efforts by many men. It has a life, a standing, a reputation, and a function to perform, however, that pertain to it alone. In a sense, all this points to future services. But we should not forget that the services which the store performs each decade have been made possible partly by the efficiency and saving of the past decade. Men of the past as well as of the present have foregone part of the dividends they might have enjoyed so that the men of the future would have the advantage of a strong stable institution. How long this building-up should go on, of course, is a moot question. There is the parable of the rich farmer and the threatened socialization of all past efforts.

§6. Education in co-operation and in business. One of the tenets of the co-operative movement is that a portion of the profits should be devoted to education in co-operative methods. President Munro did a little to educate the members in the actual procedures and results of the Society's operation but gave it up when it seemed ineffective and when the directors thought the effort not worth the cost. I refer to full annual statements printed with the Treasurer's Reports. But there has been no effort to inculcate any ideas or ideals of a social nature that might underlie the movement.

One of the difficulties in educating the members or the public is the indifference that comes from success. Half wreck the Society, and there would be plenty of interest. Reduce the dividend by 4 per cent and there would be a demand for information.

At this point it is necessary to revert to the ticket-holders (that is, members under the constitution or by-laws of 1903). Once a year they have held their meetings. On these occasions the minutes of the last meeting are read, or the reading is omitted. Then the printed report of the board of directors is read. The secretary points out that there are apparently no nominations for officers and directors, except those made by the (board of) stockholders, which are thereupon placed on file. Then adjournment takes place. The total time occupied has commonly been about 10 minutes.

The average attendance of the ticket-holders' meetings has been as follows:

1903–11 — average attendance		....	6.2
1912–19 —	"	"	3.6
1920–37 —	"	"	4.0
1938–40 —	"	"	11.0

At the meeting in 1931 there were two seniors and three officers present for a 10 minutes' session. In 1939 there were 5 undergraduates and 4 others present. Three suggestions were made and numerous questions were asked. In 1940 there were 18 persons present, 5 being officers. This meeting had been announced beforehand in 3 issues of the *Crimson*, in accordance with a suggestion for greater publicity made in the previous meeting. The time occupied was 75 minutes, during which a call was made for a history of the Co-operative. The resolution reads as follows: "that a booklet be issued to give the History, Organization and General Business policies of the Harvard Co-operative Society, the opportunities for members to take part and the willingness of the management to co-operate." The most active student in the meetings of both 1939 and 1940 was Mr. W. H. Kruskal, who was graduated in 1940 and entered the Graduate School of Arts and Sciences the same year.

Following the meeting of the ticket-holders in 1939 had come a vote of the board of directors in favor of a history and the appointment of a committee to prepare a statement concerning such a history. "It was the sense of the meeting that some statement might be prepared which would afford interesting information for Participating Members and others making inquiries concerning the business and policy of the Harvard Co-operative Society, Inc."

Quite clearly there was no thought of propaganda or education in co-operation along general lines. Information about the Society was all that was called for. At Technology there was being made a similar request for information. In the midst of all this I stepped into the manager's office one day in 1941 to ask whether he could give me a pamphlet that would set forth the history. Within a few months I was asked to undertake the compilation of the material for a history. Having supervised the collection of important facts and being unable to find in the midst of the gathering war anyone to do the actual writing, I undertook the job myself. The Co-operative has financed the collection of materials and the publication.

As we have already seen, the Society has either rejected or abandoned some of the principles usually followed by co-operatives, namely,

1. Democratic control,
2. Sales exclusively for cash,
3. Use of a portion of the profits for education in co-operation,
4. Co-operation with other co-operative societies.

But this does not mean that the Society has been doing nothing for education in business. It has provided for the participation in business of the following groups: (a) four undergraduates sitting on the board of directors, (b) a few mere professors participating in the work of the board of directors and of the (board of) stockholders, and (c) several administrative professors and non-faculty officials, already experienced in charitable administration, participating in the administration of a business that is devoted to service and to dividends. For the rank and file of us, the Society has provided, above all, a fine example of an institution devoted to service, moderate prices, dividends, progress, and stability. So that we may the better understand how to use the Society's services and perhaps develop a means of improving them, I append a set of specific questions and answers.

QUESTIONS AND ANSWERS

1. How many companies are found in the Harvard Co-operative Society? Only two — the unincorporated partnership of 1882–1903 and the corporation beginning in 1903.

2. How does one tell them apart? They have the same title, except that the corporation often adds the word "Inc."

3. Do the two exist today? Yes.

4. Which is the more important? The corporation.

5. What does the unincorporated partnership or association do? The ticket-holders, who constitute the personnel, get together once a year in the Ticket-holders' (or Participating Members') Meeting held in October.

6. What do they accomplish? Practically nothing.

7. What might they do? They might elect the officers and other directors of the Society, if 25 members would nominate these and if at least 10 per cent of the ticket-holders or participating members who are students or officers of Harvard should assemble and vote. In 1941–42 this would have involved a meeting of at least 614, with all voting. In other words, it would take about 308 votes to elect anyone. What a town meeting!

8. Is it possible to have the ticket-holders ever elect the officers and other directors? Yes, possible but not practical.

9. Then who does elect the officers and other directors? The (board of) stockholders — 10 men co-optatively chosen — elect them.

10. Where did the stockholders come from? They were provided by the constitution (or by-laws) of 1903, which in turn was formulated in accordance with a majority vote of the existing members of the Society.

11. Who chooses the manager? The board of directors.

12. Who selects and dismisses the employees? The manager.

13. What classes of "members" are there in the Society? There are two main classes: (a) the 10 stockholders (in prac-

tice members) who hold the stock as trustees and (b) the other ticket-holders who have certain rights. In 1941–42 these ticket-holders numbered 15,865.

14. Who are the ticket-holders? Those "members" who pay their annual fees and subscribe to the by-laws.

15. Are the ticket-holders all alike? No, there are two classes: (a) those who are students and officers of Harvard and have the right to vote for officers and other directors (though they do not exercise that right), and (b) all the others.

16. Who are all the others? Harvard alumni, all connected with Harvard other than students and officers, and members of Radcliffe College, the Episcopal Theological School, and the Massachusetts Institute of Technology.

17. Is the Harvard Co-operative Society a true co-operative? There is no one definition of a true co-operative.

18. Wherein is the Society clearly a co-operative? In so far as it freely allows persons in certain groups to belong on the payment of a small fee, and it permits them to buy goods at market prices, on which patronage refunds or dividends are regularly paid once a year.

19. Wherein is the Society not so clearly a co-operative? In so far as its sales are not for cash only, in so far as the democratic voting feature is held in reserve and not used in practice, and in so far as it sells to non-members as well as to members.

20. What has been the Society's weakness? It has trained a very small number of persons in its governing processes and it has done little to make known its history, organization, policy, and management. Moreover, its constitution is a model of obscurity.

21. What has been the Society's strength? It has chosen able policy-formulators and, in recent years, has had a first-rate manager; it has put itself into an excellent financial position.

22. Why has there been so little interest among the rank and file of ticket-holders in the administration of the Society? Partly because the constitution is so involved, partly because

there is little available literature concerning the Society, and partly because the existing administration is so successful.

23. Is the Society's Main Store a true department store? Yes, if we mean (a) that all goods are carefully grouped into divisions for accounting control, (b) that there are departmental heads and subordinates, and (c) that there is initiative on the part of the heads in buying and handling goods.

24. Are the officers and directors paid? Emphatically, *yes*, though the amounts in all cases must be regarded as small, when we consider the amount of business transacted.

25. Who is the highest-paid official? The manager.

26. Why is the manager paid a good salary? Because he is little short of a genius in management. He is successful in holding the three stores together as a single organization, in getting an adequate gross margin of profit, and in keeping down expenses so that the net profit will be considerable.

27. Who is the next best-paid official? The vice-president.

28. Why does the vice-president stand so high? His remuneration just happens to come next to the manager's; in truth, it is very small. As vice-president, he is paid at about the lowest rate acceptable for such work. That a counsel is continuously necessary in merchandising is symptomatic of the times in which we live.

29. How can I get most out of the Co-operative? By joining each year and by buying as much as convenient at the Society's stores.

30. Must I pay cash? No, monthly charge accounts are arranged on filing a bond for $200 or on maintaining a constant deposit of $50 — in the case of students. But note that on charge accounts you will probably receive 2 per cent less dividend.

31. If the Society has three stores, which one shall I patronize? If resident near Harvard Square or attending lectures there, use the Main Store. Elsewhere, use your own branch, as far as it meets your needs; thereafter the Main Store.

32. Do I get dividends from purchases in all three stores?

Yes, if you are a member, if your purchase is 25 cents or over, and if you do not charge your purchases and then leave them too long unpaid.

33. What shall I do, if the Co-operative does not carry what I want? Ask the clerks and they will help you by ordering it or by getting you an order on an affiliated store, where you can make your purchases, having them charged to the Co-operative to which you make payment. Such purchases count for dividends.

34. Are the prices at the Co-operative reasonable? Yes, they are the local market prices, generally approximating those in Boston.

35. Just what do I get for my dollar in joining the Co-operative? A little handbook that lists all the college games and vacations; also the right to a dividend on your own purchases (last year 12 per cent on cash purchases), the right to purchase from affiliated retailers (and get the Society's dividend), and the right to attend the annual Ticket-holders' (or Participating Members') Meeting.

36. Is this all? No, there is also the right to have checks cashed and documents attested by a notary public, both free of charge.

37. Should I go out and boost the Society? By no means; just tell classmates and others that they are lucky in being able to join.

38. To whom should I go for further information concerning the three stores of the Society? To Mr. George E. Cole, manager of the Society (mezzanine floor, Main Store).

39. Why is Mr. Cole's name not made known, for instance, in the Society's annual handbook? Because Mr. Cole suffers from false modesty.

40. If Mr. Cole cannot answer my questions concerning the constitution, to whom should I go? The last resort is the deity or the vice-president, Austin W. Scott, professor of Law.

41. If the deity is not at home, what shall I do? Go to Professor Scott.

APPENDICES

APPENDICES

1. PRESIDENTS, 1882–1942

Mr. Frank Bolles ('82, Law)	1882–83
Prof. John W. White (Greek)	1883 (Feb.–Dec.)
Prof. Charles R. Lanman (Sanskrit)	1883–84 (pro tempore, 3 weeks)
Prof. James B. Ames (Law)	1884–90
Prof. Frank W. Taussig (Econ.)	1890–94
Asst. Prof. Edward Cummings (Soc.)	1894–95
Prof. Frank W. Taussig (Econ.)	1895–97
Prof. Eugene Wambaugh (Law)	1897–99
Asst. Prof. Edward Cummings (Soc.)	1899–1900
Asst. Prof. Lewis J. Johnson (C.Eng.)	1900–02
Instructor Charles H. Ayres, Jr. ('98, Physics)	1902–05
Mr. Arthur A. Ballantine ('04, Law)	1905–06
Asst. Prof. and Prof. William B. Munro (Gov.)	1906–18
Asst. Dean Lincoln F. Schaub (Law, S. of Bus.)	1918–19
Prof. William B. Munro (Gov.)	1919–22
Mr. Henry S. Thompson ('99, Business)	1921–22

2. VICE-PRESIDENTS, 1919–1942

Asst. Dean Lincoln F. Schaub (Law, in S. of Bus.)	1919–21
Mr. Henry S. Thompson ('99, Business)	1922–
Prof. Austin W. Scott (Law)	1922–

3. SECRETARIES, 1882–1942

Mr. Charles H. Kip ('83)	1882–83
Mr. Allen Curtis ('84)	1883–84
Mr. Herbert D. Hale ('88)	1884–87
Mr. Arthur V. Woodworth ('91)	1887–90
Mr. Thomas W. Lamont ('92)	1890–91
Mr. Charles H. Fiske ('93)	1891–92
Mr. William W. Cutler ('94)	1892–94

Mr. Shirley E. Johnson ('95) 1894–95
Mr. Luther W. Mott ('96) 1895–97
Mr. William E. Weaver ('98, Law) 1897–1901
Instructor Hugo R. Meyer ('92, Econ.) 1901–02
Prof. John H. Gardiner ('85, Eng.) 1902–05
Instructor William B. Munro ('99, Gov.) 1905–06
Instructor James A. Field ('03, Econ.) 1906–08
Mr. Arthur A. Ballantine ('04, Law) 1908–18
Mr. Walter Humphreys ('97, Sec., M.I.T.) 1918–

4. TREASURERS, 1882–1942

Mr. Henry G. Chapman, Jr. ('83) 1882–83
Mr. Thomas M. Osborne ('84) 1883–84
Mr. William H. Baldwin ('85) 1884–85
Not found 1885–86
Mr. George P. Furber ('87) 1886–88
Instructor John H. Gray ('87) 1888–89
Prof. Edward L. Mark (Anatomy) 1889–90
Office abolished (13 Nov., 1890). Work
 of treasurer combined with that of
 secretary. (See list of secretaries) 1890–1902
Mr. William M. McInnes ('85, asst. bursar,
 Harv.) 1902–11
Mr. John L. Taylor (asst. contr., then auditor,
 Harv.) 1911–40
Mr. Horace S. Ford (treas., M.I.T.) 1940–

5. SUPERINTENDENTS, 1882–1942

Arthur A. Waterman ('85) 1882–90
Charles D. Lyford 1890–99
F. H. Thomas 1899–1903
Frederick A. Laws ('97) 1903–11
M. H. Goodwin 1911–14
George E. Cole (Clark, '11) [1] 1915–
 Manager since 1919

---

[1] Mr. Cole was expense manager, Nov. 7, 1912, to Oct., 1913; managing director, Oct., 1913, to Mar. 31, 1914, while Goodwin was superintendent. Returned from absence, Jan. 1, 1915, as superintendent and *ex officio* director. In 1919 the old title of superintendent was abandoned in favor of the term manager (*ex officio* director).

6. DIRECTORS, 1882-1942

Condition of the records, especially during the early and middle years, makes accuracy impossible in some cases. Some persons elected but not serving have been omitted. *Ex officio* directors excluded.

S — Harv. student	TS — Tech. student
F — Harv. faculty	TF — Tech. faculty
A — Harv. alumnus	TA — Tech. alumnus
Ad — Harv. administrator	TAd — Tech. administrator

(Alumnus — holder of Harv. or Tech. degree)

Charles R. Lanman, F ... 1882–85
T. C. Williams, S 1882–83
John W. Suter, S 1882–83
Josiah Quincy, S 1882–83
Thaddeus D. Kenneson, S 1882–84
Henry E. Warner, S 1882–83
Herbert M. Lloyd, S ... 1882–84
Hollis Webster, S 1882–84
E. J. Sartelle, S 1882–83
Charles Eliot, S 1882
John H. Storer, S 1882–83
E. A. St. John, S 1882
James B. Ludlow, S 1882
John E. Maude, S 1882–83
Thomas H. Cabot, S 1882–83
Edward E. Rand, S 1883
Charles H. Atkinson, S .. 1883–84
Frank Bolles, S 1883–84
Frank W. Taussig, F 1883–89
Arthur A. Waterman, S .. 1883–84
Frederic Almy, S 1883–84
Francis S. Parker, S 1883–84
Edward T. Cabot, S 1884–86
James S. Russell, S 1884–87
Arthur G. Hatch, S 1884–89
William B. Noble, S 1884–85
William H. Baldwin, S .. 1885
James L. Laughlin, F 1886–88
Robert D. Smith, S 1886–89
Fred B. Lund, S 1886–88
George T. Keyes, S 1886–90
Russell Tyson, S 1886–91

Charles H. Grandgent, F . 1888–89
               1897–98
Albert B. Hart, F 1889–93
Charles D. Wetmore, S .. 1889–90
William C. Forbes, S 1889–90
Frederick C. de Sumich-
    rast, F 1889–90
               1894–97
Charles R. Nutter, S ... 1889–90
M. Chamberlain, F (?) .. 1890–91
James A. Bailey, S 1890–91
Guy H. Holliday, S 1890–92
Horace A. Davis, S 1890–92
Thomas W. Lamont, S .. 1890
Conrad H. Slade, S 1890–91
Morris H. Morgan, F 1890–91
Joshua C. Hubbard, S ... 1890–91
Ledyard Heckscher, S ... 1890–91
Albert A. Howard, F ... 1891–94
Augustus N. Hand, S ... 1891–92
Arthur H. Lockett, S 1891–92
Samuel C. Davis, S 1891–94
Kinney Smith, S 1891–92
William W. Cutler, S 1891–92
W. S. Hockley, S 1892–94
James K. Whittemore, S . 1892–94
Arthur H. Brewer, S 1892–94
Frederick B. Campbell, S . 1892–94
John C. Breckinridge, S .. 1892–94
Joseph Allen, S 1893–94
Edward Cummings, F ... 1893–94
William N. Bates, S 1894–95

Bertram G. Waters, S ... 1894–95
Clyde A. Duniway, SF .. 1894–97
Luther W. Mott, S 1894–95
Ingersoll Bowditch, S ... 1894–97
Frank B. Mallory, F ... 1895–1903
Jacob R. Crocker, S 1895–98
William B. Hutton, S 1895–97
Charles Boucher, S 1895–96
Harold B. Hayden, S 1896–99
Eugene Wambaugh, F ... 1896–97
Willis Munro, S 1897–98
William B. Cutting, S ... 1897–98
Allerton S. Cushman, S . 1897–98
J. M. Boutwell, S 1898–1901
Charles H. Ayres, S ... 1899–1901
R. C. Davis, S 1898–1900
Walter P. Eaton, S 1898–99
Joseph H. A. Symonds, S 1898–99
William Phillips, S 1899–1900
John R. Locke, S 1899–1901
Barrett Wendell, Jr., S . 1899–1902
Francis R. Dickinson, S . 1900–01
Hugo R. Meyer, F 1900–01
J. B. Hayward, S 1900
Roger Ernst, S 1901–03
Michael A. Sullivan, S ... 1901–02
Jens I. Westengard, F . 1901–03
Arthur A. Ballantine, S .. 1901–05
Stanley Cunningham, S .. 1901–02
John H. Gardiner, F 1901–02
Kenneth L. Mark, S 1902–03
James A. Burgess, S ... 1902–04
R. W. Leatherbee, S 1902–03
Charles L. Bouton, F 1902–10
Walter B. Cannon, F 1903–14
Howard L. Blackwell, FAd 1903–24
Grenville Clark, S 1903–06
Raymond H. Oveson, S .. 1903–08
Charles D. Morgan, S ... 1903–08
John Reynolds, Jr., S ... 1904–07
George G. Ball, S 1905–06
Payson Dana, S 1906–07
Henry S. Blair, S 1906–08

Shaun Kelly, S 1906–08
James Ford, S 1907–09
Willard P. Fuller, S 1907–09
Arthur S. Johnson, A ... 1908–10
Nicholas Kelley, S 1908–09
Lawrence K. Lunt, S 1908–09
George E. Jones, Jr., S ... 1908–11
Richard B. Gregg, S 1909–11
Pierre W. Saxton, S 1909–10
Robert L. Groves, S 1909–10
Richard B. Wigglesworth,
  S 1909–11
Frederick A. Laws, Sup't . 1909–11[a]
Lincoln F. Schaub, F 1910–18
Henry S. Thompson, A .. 1910–21
Carroll Dunham, S 1910–11
Daniel Sargent, S 1910–12
Alexander Wheeler, S ... 1911–13
Arthur Beane, SA 1911–19
Robert W. Williams, S ... 1911–12
Charles P. Curtis, S 1911–12
M. H. Goodwin, Sup't ... 1911–14[a]
George N. Phillips, S 1912–14
Quentin Reynolds, S 1912–13
J. C. Talbot, S 1912–15
W. C. Brown, S 1913–17
Wells Blanchard, S 1913–14
Francis H. Cabot, Jr., S . 1914–17
Kent Bromley, S 1914–16
Major Edwin T. Cole, TF 1916–19
Charles P. Reynolds, S .. 1916–17
Henry C. Flower, S 1916–17
Walter Humphreys, TA .. 1917–18
John G. Coolidge, 2nd, S 1917–18
Henry V. Fox, S 1917–18
E. J. Brehaut, S 1917–18
Cass Canfield, S 1917–18
Robert W. Van Kirk, Jr.,
  TS 1917–18
Kenneth Reid, TS 1918
Homer V. Howes, TS ... 1918–20
Douglas J. Grant, S 1918–19
Henry Fay, TF 1919–20

[a] Attended meetings but probably without a vote.

Horace S. Ford, TAd ...1919–40
Edward R. Gay, Ad 1919–23
Frederic K. Bullard, S ...1919–20ᵇ
Frederic C. Church, S ...1919–20ᵇ
M. P. Baker, S 1919–20ᵇ
Edward C. Storrow, Jr., S 1920–21
George V. S. Smith, S ...1920–21
Bertram K. Little, S 1920–23
Maurice G. Townend, TS .1920–21
Henry J. Horn, Jr., TS ..1921–22
W. J. Brocker, S 1921–22
H. P. Bullard, S 1921–24
Donald K. David, FAd ..1921–26
Jasper Whiting, TF 1921–41
Austin W. Scott, F 1921–22
Alfred C. Redfield, F ...1923–
Roscoe H. Smith, TS ...1922–23
W. E. Stillwell, Jr., S 1922–25
Delmar Leighton, FAd ...1923–
C. M. Wells, Jr., S 1923–24
Douglas F. Elliott, TS ...1923–24
Fred W. Moore, S 1924–27
George H. Stark, TS 1924–25
Donald Le B. Sweeney, S 1924–27
John R. Barry, S 1924–27
Edgar F. Stevens, TS 1925–26
Ralph G. Luttmann, S ..1925–27
H. G. Crosby, S 1926–27
James L. Pool, S 1926–28
Clinton P. Biddle, FAd ..1927–38
Elisha Gray, TS 1927–28
Kenneth B. Murdock, FAd 1927–
James Roosevelt, S 1927–28
Richard A. Stout, S 1927–30

Fisher Hills, TS 1928–30
William P. Lage, S 1928–30
F. H. Gade, S 1928–31
Robert N. Clark, Jr., TS 1929–32
Edmund G. Blake, TS ..1929–30
B. K. Bachrach, S 1930–33
Oscar Goodhand, TS ...1930–31
Theodore Chase, S 1931–34
Carroll L. Wilson, TSA ..1931–32
                        1936–
E. F. Bowditch, S 1932–35
Wilber B. Huston, TS ..1932–33
Henry N. Karr, TS 1933–34
R. S. Playfair, S 1933–36
John B. Ballard, TS 1934–35
C. C. Gibson, S 1934–37
Francis Keppel, S. 1935–38
Elwood H. Koontz, S 1935–36
J. D. Andrews, S 1936–39
William J. McCune, Jr.,
  TS 1936–37
Thomas V. Healey, S 1937–40
Willard Roper, TS 1937–38
D. D. Henry, S. 1938–41
Oswald Steward, 2nd, TS 1938–39
John W. Ballantine, S ...1939–
John H. Holloman, S 1939–40
Stanley F. Teele, F 1939–
William M. Folberth, Jr.,
  S 1940–
Ralph E. Freeman, TF ..1940–
George E. Putnam, S 1940–
Carl E. Wenk, Jr., TS...1941–
George A. Saxton, Jr., S .1941–

7. STOCKHOLDERS, 1902–1942

F   — Harv. faculty   TAd — Tech. administrator
Ad — Harv. administrator   R   — Radcliffe
TF — Tech. faculty

Henry L. Higginson, Ad .1902–07   Samuel Williston, F 1902–06
Le Baron R. Briggs, FAd .1902–05ᵃ   Wallace C. Sabine, FAd ..1902–19

ᵇ Did not attend any meetings.

ᵃ If Dean Briggs served during 1904–05, there were 6 stockholders instead of 5.

Harold C. Ernst, F 1902-03
A. Lawrence Lowell, F ..1903-08
Jerome D. Greene, Ad ..1904-10
Bruce Wyman, F 1906-14
Edwin F. Gay, FAd 1907-19
Benjamin O. Peirce, F ..1908-14
Charles H. Haskins, FAd 1910-22
F. Lowell Kennedy, F ...1914-36
Henry A. Yeomans, FAd .1914-34
George C. Whipple, F ...1916-25
Felix Frankfurter, F 1916-27
Davis R. Dewey, TF ...1916-33
Chester N. Greenough,
   FAd 1916-38
Charles C. Lane, FAd ...1916-19
Austin W. Scott, F 1919-21
Elmer P. Kohler, FAd ..1919-38
Wallace B. Donham, FAd 1920-
Chester A. McLain, F ...1921-23

Edward F. Miller, TF ...1922-33
John M. Maguire, F 1923-41
John W. Lowes, Ad 1925-33
William B. Munro, F 1927-30
Wilbur C. Abbott, F 1930-32
Alfred C. Hanford, FAd .1932-
Harold E. Lobdell, TFAd 1933-
Erwin H. Schell, TF 1933-
Richard W. Thorpe, RAd 1933-
Edward A. Whitney, FAd 1934-39
Donald H. McLaughlin, F 1936-41
Edmund M. Morgan, F ..1938-
John T. Murray, FAd ...1938-39
Arthur B. Lamb, FAd ...1939-
William J. Bingham, Ad .1939-
Andrew J. Casner, F 1941-
Francis T. Spaulding, FAd 1941
Keyes D. Metcalf, Ad ...1942-

8. BROAD CLASSIFICATION OF MEMBERSHIP, 1882–1942 [a]

(1) Year	(2) Total Members	(3) Unclassified and Alumni Members	(4) Teachers and Students Members	(5) Teachers and Students Qualified [b]	(6) Teachers and Students not Members	
					No.	%
1881–82......	....	....	....	1,570	....	...
1882–83......	713	[e]	713	1,624	911	56.1 [d]
1883–84......	[750] [e]	....	[750] [e]	1,841	1,091	59.2
1884–85......	790	....	790	1,881	1,091	58.0
1885–86......	....	....	....	1,972	....	...
1886–87......	....	....	....	2,057	....	...
1887–88......	....	....	....	2,278	....	...
1888–89......	[621]	....	[621]	2,422	1,801	74.4
1889–90......	[762]	....	[762]	2,710	1,948	71.8
1890–91......	[987]	....	[987]	3,025	2,038	60.7
1891–92......	1,299	....	1,299	3,555	2,256	63.4
1892–93......	[989]	....	[989]	4,072	3,083	75.7
1893–94......	1,681	....	1,681	4,138	2,457	59.3
1894–95......	1,909	....	1,909	4,459	2,550	56.7
1895–96......	2,252	....	2,252	4,957	2,705	54.5
1896–97......	2,380	....	2,380	5,108	2,728	53.4
1897–98......	2,308	....	2,308	5,446	3,138	57.6
1898–99......	2,304	....	2,304	5,536	3,232	58.3
1899–1900....	2,471	....	2,471	5,854	3,383	57.8
1900–01......	2,671	....	2,671	6,274	3,603	57.4
1901–02......	2,673	....	2,673	6,105	3,432	56.2
1902–03......	2,895	....	2,895	6,220	3,325	53.4
1903–04......	2,576	....	2,576	6,394	3,818	59.7
1904–05......	2,513	....	2,513	5,829	3,316	56.8
1905–06......	2,162	....	2,162	5,767	3,605	62.5
1906–07......	2,187	180 [f]	2,007	5,871	3,864	65.8
1907–08......	2,479	252	2,227	5,823	3,596	61.7
1908–09......	2,493	250	2,243	6,042	3,799	62.5
1909–10......	2,700	285	2,415	6,330	3,915	61.8
1910–11......	2,754	348	2,406	6,137	3,731	60.8
1911–12......	2,844	463	2,381	6,305	3,924	62.2
1912–13......	3,037	510	2,527	6,589	4,062	61.6
1913–14......	3,193	597	2,596	5,770	3,174	55.0
1914–15......	3,255	662	2,593	7,069	4,476	63.3
1915–16......	3,196	681	2,515	7,728	5,213	67.4
1916–17......	5,035	676 [g]	4,359	10,747	6,388	59.4
1917–18......	3,871	582	3,289	7,655	4,366	57.0
1918–19......	3,887	565	3,322	8,248	4,926	59.7
1919–20......	6,375	822	5,553	12,392	6,839	55.2
1920–21......	7,374	880	6,494	12,690	6,196	48.8

8. Broad Classification of Membership, 1882–1942 [a] (continued)

(1) Year	(2) Total Members	(3) Unclassified and Alumni Members	(4) Teachers and Students Members	(5) Teachers and Students Qualified [b]	(6) Teachers and Students not Members	
1921–22	7,932	725	7,207	13,528	6,321	46.7
1922–23	8,388	885	7,503	13,974	6,471	46.3
1923–24	9,073	1,033	8,040	14,202	6,162	43.3
1924–25	9,943	1,241	8,702	14,677	5,975	40.7
1925–26	10,800	1,436 [h]	9,364	15,423	6,059	39.3
1926–27	11,339	1,489	10,850	15,844	4,994	31.5
1927–28	12,007	1,635	10,372	16,438	6,066	36.8
1928–29	12,537	1,512	11,025	16,562	5,537	33.4
1929–30	13,011	1,502	11,509	17,094	5,585	32.6
1930–31	13,183	1,405	11,733	17,532	5,799	33.0
1931–32	13,032	1,528	11,504	17,887	6,383	35.0
1932–33	11,827	1,402	10,425	16,302	5,877	36.0
1933–34	10,867	1,364	9,503	15,217	5,714	37.5
1934–35	10,631	1,477	9,154	15,067	5,913	39.2
1935–36	11,178	1,575	9,603	15,541	5,938	38.2
1936–37	12,396	1,759	10,637	16,731	6,094	36.4
1937–38	13,024	2,042	10,982	17,001	6,019	35.4
1938–39	13,668	2,348	11,320	17,928	6,608	36.7
1939–40	13,928	2,248	11,680	17,503	5,823	33.2
1940–41	14,345	2,577	11,768	17,551	5,783	32.9
1941–42	14,248 [i]	2,755 [j]	11,493	16,317	4,824	29.5

[a] This table is necessarily incomplete and unsatisfactory. Still the figures, where not exact, are not far out; and the trends are accurate. Column 5 is accurate; column 2 is uncertain only in the early years; column 3 is fragmentary as indicated in the footnotes below.

Column 4 is column 2 minus column 3. Column 6 is column 5 minus column 4.

[b] Enrolled in Harvard University, Radcliffe College, Episcopal Theological School, and the Massachusetts Institute of Technology.

[c] No figures for 1882–83 — 1905–06. This gap impairs the validity of columns 4 and 6 for these years, particularly from about 1901 onward.

[d] The figures in this sub-column represent the percentage that column 6 is of column 5.

[e] Estimates in [ ].

[f] Exact figures 1906–07 to 1915–16 inclusive.

[g] Figures for 1916–17 to 1924–25 include unclassified and alumni members only from Harvard. Thus the figures in columns 4 and 6 are somewhat too high for these years.

[h] From 1925–26 onward, there is only a slight element of uncertainty. "Graduates" of Technology have been divided, 80 per cent being regarded as graduate students and 20 per cent as alumni.

[i] The total number of members is really 15,865, but this includes 1,617 defense workers, who for the purpose of this table are extraneous.

[j] Includes 146 Technology alumni isolated for the first time.

9. OPERATION AND FINANCES, 1882–1942

Year	Sales of Goods and Services	Membership Dues	Net Profits Available for Dividends	Dividends [a]	Available for Capital and Surplus	Capital and Surplus
1882–83	$ 15,600.87[b]	$ 1,163.00	$ 121.74(?)	None	......	$ 363.87[c]
1883–84	18,230.23	1,314.00	−594.53(?)	None	......	......
1884–85	16,032.13	1,975.00	711.81	None	......	779.10[d]
1885–86	27,000.00	......	......	None	......	......
1886–87	31,970.91	......	1.73	$ 1,493.00	......	3,057.00
1887–88	60,000.00(?)	......	2.86	2,150.00	......	4,132.00
1888–89	68,976.12	931.50	2,800.08	1,723.08	$ 1,077.00	4,714.81
1889–90	66,521.94	1,143.00	3,409.33	2,045.60	1,363.73	5,851.25
1890–91	70,734.84	1,480.50	4,763.74	2,800.00	1,963.74[e]	7,814.99[f]
1891–92	95,415.44	1,948.50	7,272.07	4,000.00	3,272.07	18,171.16[g]
1892–93	106,934.13	1,484.00	7,631.43	5,000.00	2,543.81	10,532.29
1893–94	118,530.65	1,681.00	7,328.95	5,000.00	2,328.95	13,076.10
1894–95	135,267.63	1,909.00	7,761.07	5,000.00	2,761.07	15,405.05
1895–96	150,572.26	2,252.00	9,071.56	6,000.00	3,071.56	18,166.12
1896–97	153,228.48	2,380.00	6,759.60	5,000.00	1,759.60	21,237.68
1897–98	162,536.37	2,308.00	7,000.03	5,000.00	2,000.03	22,997.28
1898–99	170,477.36	2,304.00	7,510.30	6,000.00	1,510.30	24,997.31
1899–1900	206,457.56	2,471.00	9,797.59	6,948.38	3,474.21	28,471.52
1900–01	246,337.49	2,671.00	12,811.04	8,692.55	4,118.49	32,374.75
1901–02	259,815.21	2,673.00	16,569.23	10,956.15	5,613.08	36,493.24
1902–03	289,218.04	2,895.00	21,566.31	12,426.33	9,139.98	42,106.32
1903–04	245,517.59	2,576.00	5,849.78	5,294.70	555.08	51,407.81[h]
1904–05	238,315.14	2,513.00	9,405.42	8,565.21	840.21	51,962.89
1905–06	249,251.44	2,162.00	10,907.85	10,740.99	166.86	52,723.10
1906–07	281,943.56	2,187.00	14,273.25	13,330.01	789.85	52,889.96

9. Operation and Finances, 1882–1942 (continued)

Year	Sales of Goods and Services	Membership Dues	Net Profits Available for Dividends	Dividends [a]	Available for Capital and Surplus	Capital and Surplus
1907–08	304,724.74	2,479.00	15,392.69	14,955.97	436.72	53,679.81
1908–09	316,123.83	2,493.00	15,303.81	15,209.24	94.57	54,116.53
1909–10	365,248.28	2,700.00	19,003.54	18,552.48	451.06	54,211.10
1910–11	378,170.14	2,754.00	18,935.14	18,557.58	377.56	54,662.16
1911–12	376,273.79	2,844.00	20,157.24	19,059.91	1,097.33	55,039.72
1912–13	418,774.19	3,037.00	19,728.26	19,493.58	27.79	56,137.05
1913–14	429,987.76	3,193.00	18,627.83	18,543.88	54.79	56,164.84
1914–15	443,820.78	3,255.00	15,202.84	15,076.74	98.77	56,219.63
1915–16	445,391.45	3,196.00	18,544.61	16,657.52	1,877.09	56,318.40
1916–17	561,101.05	5,035.00	22,822.64	19,612.73	15,710.39	58,205.49
1917–18	479,361.20	3,871.00	16,127.31	15,335.79	8,972.35	73,915.88
1918–19	560,828.20	3,887.00	19,200.00	18,790.40	2,509.85	82,888.23
1919–20	874,111.48	6,375.00	40,135.67	39,418.20	9,445.63	85,398.08
1920–21	907,071.17	7,374.00	42,013.28	42,411.12	11,558.54	94,843.71
1921–22	829,193.63	7,932.00	43,896.37	43,988.22	7,619.52	106,402.25
1922–23	831,864.61	8,388.00	48,420.96	47,441.07	7,375.73	114,021.77
1923–24	909,406.56	9,073.00	100,426.00	53,300.38	129,286.78	121,397.50
1924–25	943,399.98	9,943.00	59,258.43	58,558.43	539.20	250,684.28 [i]
1925–26	1,085,467.71	10,800.00	70,527.70	70,198.34	166.42	251,223.48
1926–27	1,181,309.27	11,339.00	84,770.18	78,384.93	72,285.61	251,389.90
1927–28	1,297,801.12	12,007.00	89,097.18	86,689.10	42,321.41	323,675.51
1928–29	1,351,692.94	12,537.00	105,864.25	89,970.22	60,330.42	365,996.92
1929–30	1,394,390.94	13,011.00	96,113.34	93,972.61	51,964.63	426,327.34
1930–31	1,354,529.33	13,183.00	94,121.44	87,153.08	6,819.71	478,291.97
1931–32	1,205,784.81	13,032.00	79,239.84	78,278.33	27,272.46	485,111.68
1932–33	947,744.85	11,827.00	56,300.00 [j]	56,060.46	18,643.41 [j]	512,384.14

1933–34.........	938,605.35	10,876.00	55,600.00	54,953.83	5,763.30	531,027.55
1934–35.........	946,187.69	10,631.00	56,000.00	55,394.62	10,586.80	536,790.85
1935–36.........	1,061,307.98	11,178.00	70,000.00	69,435.86	−1,405.76	547,377.65
1936–37.........	1,233,191.93	12,396.00	83,500.00	82,894.15	−9,768.41	545,971.89
1937–38.........	1,267,451.48	13,024.00	106,288.05	84,511.57	29,579.18	536,203.48
1938–39.........	1,268,058.23	13,668.00	88,406.15	85,713.23	12,653.29	565,782.66
1939–40.........	1,327,473.79	13,928.00	116,746.10	109,333.89	90,024.56 k	578,435.95
1940–41.........	1,420,306.92	14,345.00	131,552.56	115,839.71	53,581.45	668,460.51
1941–42.........	1,639,325.76	15,865.00	186,786.63	133,205.18	51,230.92	722,041.96
Total...........	34,778,938.33	345,897.50	2,296,642.28	2,055,118.35	......	......

ª Discrepancies occur because the only available figures sometimes represent dividends declared and sometimes dividends paid.

ᵇ Otherwise $14,763.87 by Feb. 16, 1883.

ᶜ "True capital" after 11 months of operation.

ᵈ As of Jan. 1, 1885.

ᵉ Another figure found is $1,593.

ᶠ On July 1, 1891, the capital was put at $6,000.

ᵍ "Society" (or capital) plus "profit and loss" (or surplus).

ʰ From this point onward, the capital is fixed at $50,000 ($45,000 for a few months in 1903), the rest being surplus.

ⁱ Heavy investment in land and buildings began in 1924–25.

ʲ Figures in these columns for 1932–33 to 1936–37 (inclusive) are doubtful — ambiguous in the annual statements. The treasurer seems to have worked backwards in determining net profits.

ᵏ Includes the increase in value of Fixed Assets amounting to $74,311.71 due to a re-valuation by the auditors.

10. EXPENSES AND PROFITS AND ALSO BALANCE AVAILABLE FOR
DIVIDENDS AND SURPLUS AS PERCENTAGES OF SALES
1882–1941 [a]

Fin'l Year Ending	Cost of Sales	Gross Profits	Operating Expenses	Net Profits from Operation	Other Income	Other Charges	Balance Available
Feb. 16, 1883......101.61	−1.61	6.04	−7.65	8.55	...	0.90
" 18, 1884...... 96.43	3.57	14.04	−10.47	7.21	...	−3.26
Sept. 18, 1884...... ...	...	...	...	...	...	...
Jan. 1, 1885...... 93.20	6.80	14.67	−7.88	12.32	...	4.44
Sept. 1885...... ...	...	...	...	...	...	...
Sept. 1886...... ...	...	...	...	...	...	...
Sept. 19, 1887...... ...	...	...	...	...	...	0.01
Mar. 1, 1888...... ...	...	...	...	...	...	0.01
Sept. 1889...... ...	...	...	2.71	1.35	...	4.06
Sept. 1890...... 86.31	13.69	10.23	3.46	1.75	...	5.21
June 30, 1891...... 84.16	15.84	11.08	4.76	2.15	...	6.91
" " 1892...... 84.20	15.80	10.10	5.70	2.08	...	7.78
" " 1893...... 84.11	15.89	10.06	5.83	1.41	...	7.24
" " 1894...... 83.58	16.42	11.59	4.83	1.44	...	6.27
" " 1895...... 83.42	16.58	12.19	4.39	1.43	...	5.82
" " 1896...... 83.08	16.92	12.32	4.60	1.52	...	6.12
" " 1897...... 85.51	14.49	11.63	2.86	1.55	...	4.41
" " 1898...... 85.30	14.70	11.81	2.89	1.42	...	4.31
" " 1899...... 84.34	15.66	12.60	3.06	1.35	...	4.41
" " 1900...... 83.91	16.09	12.54	3.55	1.20	...	5.05
" " 1901...... 83.28	16.72	12.60	4.12	1.08	...	5.20
" " 1902...... 81.63	18.37	13.02	5.35	1.03	...	6.38
" " 1903...... 81.72	18.28	10.64	7.64	2.51	2.60	7.55
" " 1904...... 85.08	14.92	12.19	2.73	3.20	3.55	2.38
July 31, 1905...... 82.43	17.57	13.03	4.54	2.39	3.06	3.87
" " 1906...... 81.45	18.55	13.90	4.65	2.41	2.68	4.38
" " 1907...... 79.90	20.10	13.92	6.18	2.41	3.51	5.08
" " 1908...... 80.47	19.53	13.91	5.62	2.05	2.62	5.05
" " 1909...... 80.14	19.86	14.28	5.58	2.52	3.26	4.84
" " 1910...... 80.39	19.61	13.66	5.95	2.28	3.03	5.20
" " 1911...... 81.62	18.38	14.04	4.34	2.57	1.90	5.01
June 30, 1912...... 78.89	21.11	14.36	6.75	1.96	3.35	5.36
" " 1913...... 80.87	19.13	14.97	4.16	2.21	1.66	4.71
" " 1914...... 81.95	18.05	15.06	2.99	2.89	1.55	4.33
" " 1915...... 81.73	18.27	15.80	2.47	1.91	0.68	3.70
" " 1916...... 81.22	18.78	13.98	4.80	1.09	1.73	4.16
" " 1917...... 80.22	19.78	13.84	5.94	1.12	2.99	4.07
" " 1918...... 78.08	21.92	15.61	6.31	1.13	4.07	3.37
" " 1919...... 77.22	22.78	15.36	7.42	1.26	5.26	3.42
" " 1920...... 79.44	20.56	13.16	7.40	2.33	5.14	4.59

June 30, 1921	78.86	21.14	14.46	6.68	2.50	4.55	4.63
" " 1922	77.60	22.40	15.92	6.48	2.98	4.17	5.29
" " 1923	75.06	24.94	18.35	6.59	4.24	5.01	5.82
" " 1924	74.22	25.78	18.49	7.29	4.18	5.54	5.93
" " 1925	75.12	24.88	19.28	5.60	4.40	3.72	6.28
" " 1926	72.94	27.06	20.42	6.64	3.81	3.95	6.50
" " 1927	72.14	27.86	20.61	7.25	3.69	3.77	7.17
" " 1928	71.97	28.03	19.72	8.31	3.70	4.53	7.48
" " 1929	71.83	28.17	19.48	8.69	3.60	4.46	7.83
" " 1930	71.83	28.17	19.72	8.46	3.63	5.20	6.89
" " 1931	72.95	27.05	20.60	6.44	3.64	3.13	6.95
" " 1932	73.69	26.31	22.31	4.00	4.15	1.58	6.57
" " 1933	73.08	26.92	23.57	3.35	4.53	1.94	5.94
" " 1934	70.59	29.41	24.10	5.31	4.79	4.18	5.92
" " 1935	70.86	29.14	24.92	4.22	4.58	2.88	5.92
" " 1936	70.04	29.96	24.19	5.77	4.26	3.43	6.60
" " 1937	69.70	30.30	22.85	7.45	4.20	4.88	6.77
" " 1938	70.49	29.51	23.24	6.27	3.77	1.67	8.37
" " 1939	70.42	29.58	23.54	6.04	3.75	2.82	6.97
" " 1940	70.51	29.49	22.49	7.00	3.78	1.99	8.79
" " 1941	70.63	29.37	21.98	7.39	3.30	1.43	9.26

[a] Compiled by Miss Evelyn H. Puffer with notes too elaborate to publish. The figures from which these percentages are taken are in many instances not the Society's figures but are separately reckoned. To a considerable extent, the figures beginning in 1903 are not strictly comparable with the earlier ones.

APPENDICES

11. BREAK-DOWN OF EXPENSES
In Percentages of Sales, 1926–1940
(1) By Functions

Year Ending Dec. 31	Administration and General	Occupancy	Publicity	Buying and Mdsg.	Direct and General Selling	Delivery	Total
1940	7.68	5.90	1.55	2.81	5.94	1.15	25.03
1939	7.89	7.06	1.49	2.76	6.01	1.05	26.26
1938	7.69	6.47	1.55	2.80	6.00	1.05	25.56
1937	7.53	5.59	1.50	2.60	6.37	1.17	24.76
1936	7.37	6.07	1.42	2.54	6.01	1.25	24.66
1935	7.82	5.85	1.54	2.76	6.25	1.32	25.54
1934	8.10	6.18	1.61	2.88	6.05	1.33	26.15
1933	8.40	6.32	1.53	2.74	5.49	1.32	25.80
1932	7.93	6.12	1.66	2.72	5.35	1.33	25.11
1931	6.11	5.21	1.53	2.39	5.28	1.19	21.71
1930	5.66	6.05	1.44	2.32	5.10	1.14	21.71
1929	5.59	5.39	1.49	2.23	4.87	1.04	20.61
1928	5.53	4.59	1.47	2.22	5.68	1.02	20.51
1927	5.70	4.88	1.41	2.19	5.75	1.07	21.00
1926	5.64	5.30	1.43	2.27	5.64	1.17	21.45

(2) By Natural Divisions

Year Ending Dec. 31	Pay-Roll	Real Estate	Advertising	Taxes a	Interest	Supplies	Services Purchased	Communication	Repairs	Depreciation	Professional Services	Total b
1940	13.45	3.65	1.05	0.70	1.64	0.84	0.64	0.64	0.25	0.46	0.23	25.03
1939	13.48	3.85	1.05	0.76	1.69	0.66	0.52	0.62	1.22	0.41	0.20	26.26
1938	13.60	4.02	1.14	0.69	1.80	0.64	0.48	0.57	0.42	0.45	0.14	25.56
1937	13.52	2.90	1.08	0.59	1.79	0.79	0.47	0.61	0.91	0.37	0.20	24.76
1936	13.01	3.07	1.00	0.27	1.68	0.78	0.44	0.57	1.36	0.27	0.21	24.66
1935	14.88	3.67	1.05	0.07	1.75	0.81	0.45	0.62	0.23	0.39	0.29	25.54
1934	14.93	3.95	1.18	0.12	1.88	0.89	0.41	0.70	0.23	0.43	0.24	26.15
1933	13.24	4.01	1.20	0.12	1.96	0.81	0.40	0.68	0.35	0.41	0.28	25.80
1932	13.81	3.55	1.33	0.10	1.88	0.78	0.42	0.61	0.23	0.83	0.24	25.11
1931	11.74	2.85	1.15	0.06	1.78	0.78	0.40	0.52	0.34	0.69	0.22	21.69
1930	11.20	3.77	1.14	0.05	1.80	0.67	0.31	0.48	0.39	0.73	0.13	21.71
1929	10.52	4.15	1.16	0.07	1.34	0.71	0.32	0.48	0.32	0.08	0.17	20.61
1928	11.08	2.68	1.19	0.05	1.54	0.67	0.34	0.49	0.48	0.66	0.17	20.51
1927	11.26	3.02	1.09	0.04	1.65	0.73	0.34	0.47	0.30	0.81	0.19	21.00
1926	11.41	3.39	1.09	0.00	1.28	0.86	0.40	0.48	0.30	0.85	0.12	21.45

a Taxes on real estate are included under real estate.
b This is a total of all the items (columns), some of which are omitted here.

12. RATE OF DIVIDENDS, 1897–1942

Year	Rate %	Year	Rate % Cash	Rate % Charge
1897	7.5	1916	9.0	7.0
1898	5.9	1917	8.0	6.0
1899	6.9	1918	8.0	6.0 [a]
1900	7.0	1919	9.0	7.0 [b]
1901	7.0	1920	10.0	8.0
1902	8.0	1921	10.0	8.0
1903	8.0	1922	10.0	8.0
1904	4.0	1923	10.0	8.0
1905	7.0	1924	10.0	8.0
1906	8.0	1925	10.0	8.0
1907	8.0	1926	10.0	8.0
1908	8.0	1927	10.0	8.0
1909	8.0	1928	10.0	8.0
1910	9.0	1929	10.0	8.0
1911	9.0	1930	10.0	8.0
1912	9.0	1931	10.0	8.0
1913	9.0	1932	10.0	8.0
1914	8.0	1933	9.0	7.0
1915	7.0	1934	9.0	7.0
		1935	9.0	7.0
		1936	10.0	8.0
		1937	10.0	8.0
		1938	10.0	8.0
		1939	10.0	8.0
		1940	12.0	10.0
		1941	12.0	10.0
		1942	12.0	10.0

[a] Dividends at Technology were 10% on both cash and charge.
[b] Dividends at Technology were 10% on cash and 8% on charge.

13. ANALYSIS OF SALES (CASH, CHARGE, INSTALLMENT) IN THE THREE STORES, 1923–1941

(In dollars)

	Main Store	Technology			Business School		Total
		Store	Barbershop	Lunch	Store	Barbershop	
1941							
Cash	575,986.83	173,093.68	12,086.65	24,307.86	36,960.35	4,857.15	827,292.52
Charge	502,876.29	58,170.88			28,782.93		589,830.10
Instal.	2,513.60	670.70					3,184.30
Total	1,081,376.72	231,935.26	12,086.65	24,307.86	65,743.28	4,857.15	1,420,306.92
1940							
Cash	551,875.43	153,005.28	11,202.05	22,166.66	39,720.86	4,886.17	782,856.45
Charge	474,269.00	46,575.49			20,172.80		541,017.29
Instal.	2,624.97	975.08					3,600.05
Total	1,028,769.40	200,555.85	11,202.05	22,166.66	59,893.66	4,886.17	1,327,473.79
1939							
Cash	519,365.68	142,433.49	11,071.80	22,510.66	44,604.46	4,942.65	744,928.74
Charge	454,988.87	47,154.29			18,261.97		520,405.13
Instal.	2,754.64	569.72					3,334.36
Total	977,109.19	190,157.50	11,071.80	22,510.66	62,866.43	4,942.65	1,268,658.23
1938							
Cash	526,353.88	133,943.79	11,288.15	19,073.70	46,944.66	4,837.40	742,441.58
Charge	456,463.46	44,106.74			18,844.65		519,414.85
Instal.	4,662.54	932.51					5,595.05
Total	987,479.88	178,983.04	11,288.15	19,073.70	65,789.31	4,837.40	1,267,451.48

1937							
Cash	550,237.90	126,006.69	10,385.30	3,504.70	40,502.87	4,673.30	735,310.76
Charge	433,457.94	42,953.83			16,607.93		493,019.70
Instal.	4,093.31	768.16					4,861.47
Total	987,789.15	169,728.68	10,385.30	3,504.70	57,110.80	4,673.30	1,233,191.93
1936							
Cash	464,272.04	108,763.61	9,567.96		29,513.90	4,068.70	616,186.21
Charge	388,827.12	39,517.30			11,821.72		440,166.14
Instal.	4,435.76	519.87					4,955.63
Total	857,534.92	148,800.78	9,567.96		41,335.62	4,068.70	1,061,307.98
1935							
Cash	411,891.44	101,467.66	8,880.60		24,254.33	3,906.51	550,400.54
Charge	341,683.36	41,957.02			10,043.96		393,684.34
Instal.	1,780.31	322.41					2,102.72
Total	755,355.11	143,747.09	8,880.60		34,298.29	3,906.51	946,187.60
1934							
Cash	403,561.84	93,733.45	8,545.90		28,253.31	4,263.17	538,357.67
Charge	345,855.98	41,135.94			13,255.76		400,247.68
Total	749,417.82	134,869.39	8,545.90		41,509.07	4,263.17	938,605.35
1933							
Cash	391,909.96	99,909.89	8,435.80		39,946.75	4,937.10	545,139.50
Charge	342,278.05	43,588.76			16,738.54		402,605.35
Total	734,188.01	143,498.65	8,435.80		56,685.29	4,937.10	947,744.85

	Main Store	Technology Store	Technology Barbershop	Lunch	Business School Store	Business School Barbershop	Total
1932							
Cash	466,823.43	129,580.92	10,913.60		56,004.13	5,884.75	669,206.83
Charge	457,166.70	56,385.05			23,026.23		536,577.98
Total	923,990.13	185,965.97	10,913.60		79,030.36	5,884.75	1,205,784.81
1931							
Cash	518,575.12	123,343.36	11,112.25		61,096.96	6,139.19	720,266.88
Charge	531,776.34	79,144.19			23,341.92		634,262.45
Total	1,050,351.46	202,487.55	11,112.25		84,438.88	6,139.19	1,354,529.33
1930							
Cash	578,215.27	140,862.05	10,347.90		60,595.95	6,892.46	796,913.63
Charge	522,061.67	51,534.55			23,881.09		597,477.31
Total	1,100,276.94	192,396.60	10,347.90		84,477.04	6,892.46	1,394,390.94
1929							
Cash	556,502.67	136,067.88	9,893.60		56,005.68	5,698.46	764,168.29
Charge	515,103.87	49,483.73			22,937.05		587,524.65
Total	1,071,606.54	185,551.61	9,893.60		78,942.73	5,698.46	1,351,692.94
1928							
Cash	549,329.71	126,943.12	9,439.35		42,106.32	4,975.20	732,793.70
Charge	498,643.54	48,977.88			17,386.00		565,007.42
Total	1,047,973.25	175,921.00	9,439.35		59,492.32	4,975.20	1,297,801.12

1927				
Cash	536,073.23	129,864.58	9,577.70	675,515.51
Charge	460,353.36	45,440.40		505,793.76
Total	996,426.59	175,304.98	9,577.70	1,181,309.27
1926				
Cash	472,993.48	137,336.31	9,789.00	620,118.79
Charge	421,194.11	44,154.81		465,348.92
Total	894,187.59	181,491.12	9,789.00	1,085,467.71
1925				
Cash	368,261.32	148,712.70	9,422.20	526,396.22
Charge	377,543.58	39,460.18		417,003.76
Total	745,804.90	188,172.88	9,422.20	943,399.98
1924				
Cash	353,228.35	154,709.60	9,616.60	517,554.55
Charge	356,211.78	35,640.23		391,852.01
Total	709,440.13	190,349.83	9,616.60	909,406.56
1923				
Cash	289,982.01	171,672.62	10,295.00	471,949.63
Charge	338,350.47	21,564.51		359,914.98
Total	628,332.48	193,237.13	10,295.00	831,864.61

14. Number of Members Classified According to the Amount of Their Annual Purchases [a]

(Every Fifth Year from 1924–25)

	Up to $25	Over $25 to $50	Over $50 to $100	Over $100 to $200	Over $200 to $300	Over $300 to $1,000	Over $1,000	No Dividend Purchases [b]	Total Members
1930–40									
Main Store	2,396	2,399	2,498	1,447	312	206	5	54	9,317
Tech.	664	1,229	1,100	387	35	22	5	5	3,442
Bus. School	167	250	401	289	41	18		3	1,169
Total No.	3,227	3,878	3,999	2,123	388	246	5	62	13,928
%	23.17	27.84	28.71	15.24	2.79	1.77	0.03	0.45	
1934–35									
Main Store	1,978	2,057	1,919	1,034	233	124	2	66	7,413
Tech.	498	910	710	200	18	3		13	2,352
Bus. School	167	237	301	118	26	10		7	866
Total No.	2,643	3,204	2,930	1,352	277	137	2	86	10,631
%	24.86	30.14	27.56	12.71	2.61	1.29	0.02	0.81	
1929–30									
Main Store	1,893	2,389	2,293	1,419	404	273	7	87	8,765
Tech.	544	1,063	976	280	28	10		12	2,913
Bus. School	172	223	380	403	105	38		12	1,333
Total No.	2,609	3,675	3,649	2,102	537	321	7	111	13,011
%	20.05	28.24	28.05	16.16	4.13	2.47	0.05	0.85	
1924–25									
Main Store	1,875	1,894	1,858	944	225	136	3	141	7,076
Tech.	566	1,020	1,012	220	26	7		16	2,867
Total No.	2,441	2,914	2,870	1,164	251	143	3	157	9,943
%	24.55	29.31	28.86	11.71	2.52	1.44	0.03	1.58	

[a] All purchases of goods or services under 25 cents bear no dividend. Such purchases are not recorded as having been made by member or non-member.

15. Number of Employees by Divisions and Departments, 1922–1942 [a]

	May '42	'37	'32	'27	'22	Sept. '42	'37	'32	'27	'22	Dec. '42	'37	'32	'27	'22
Main Store:															
Office	17	13	9	11	8	23	17	15	14	8	20	13	10	12	8
Men's Furnishings	7	5	3	4	5	10	7	4	5	5	12	10	5	7	5
Ready to Wear	5	6	3	4	..	8	7	4	3	..	4	4	3	4	..
Books	6	6	4	5	5	23	20	21	17	11	11	14	9	12	5
Stationery	16	15	7	10	6	37	36	24	16	9	35	18	14	16	9
House Furnishings	4	3	3	4	4	17	18	10	11	13	10	15	10	9	10
Ski	..	..	..	..	..	..	..	..	..	..	10	6	..	..	..
Shipping Room	12	7	8	9	8	19	12	11	10	8	10	11	10	10	8
Drivers	5	5	4	4	4	5	6	5	4	4	6	5	5	4	3
Maintenance	7	6	4	4	2	7	6	5	5	2	7	6	5	5	2
Manufacturing — Tailoring	17	18	17	17	20	16	16	17	17	16	17	16	16	17	20
Total	96	84	62	72	62	165	145	116	102	76	143	118	87	96	70
Business School															
Store	9	3	2	..	..	14	13	8	..	..	5	3	2	..	..
Barbershop	5	5	3	..	..	4	5	4	..	..	4	5	4	..	..
Total	14	8	5	..	..	18	18	12	..	..	9	8	6	..	..
Technology															
Store	17	17	5	9	12	31	25	22	28	25	16	13	7	12	10
Barbershop	5	5	4	4	4	5	5	4	4	4	5	5	4	4	4
Luncheonette	7	..	..	..	..	9	..	..	..	..	7	..	..	..	..
Total	29	22	9	13	16	45	30	26	32	29	28	18	11	16	14
Managers and asst. managers of depts.	22	20	21	18	14	23	19	20	18	14	23	19	18	18	14
Total	161	134	97	103	92	251	212	174	152	119	203	163	122	130	98

[a] The year given is 1 July to 30 June. Thus, 1942 is July 1, 1941, to June 30, 1942.

16. NUMBER OF EMPLOYEES [a] AND THEIR PERFORMANCE, 1926–1940

Year Ending Dec. 31	Selling-employees [b]	Non-selling-employees [c]	Total	Selling-employee % of Total	Total No. of Transactions [d]	Transactions per Selling-employee	Net Sales per Selling-employee	Size of Sales (Gross) [e]
1940	62	86	148	41.89	1,031,992	16,645	$22,054	$1.35
1939	60	85	145	41.38	960,222	16,004	21,417	1.36
1938	50	73	123	40.65	921,207	18,424	25,224	1.37
1937	47	53	100	47.00	830,843	17,678	26,794	1.52
1936	43	48	91	47.25	729,137	16,957	27,254	1.61
1935	40	46	86	46.51	656,490	16,412	24,863	1.51
1934	38	44	82	46.34	621,462	16,354	24,644	1.51
1933	36	43	79	45.57	624,414	17,345	25,631	1.48
1932	37	46	83	44.58	700,942	18,944	28,186	1.49
1931	52	38	90	57.78			24,925	
1930	53	38	91	58.24			25,800	
1929	54	38	92	58.70			25,710	
1928	:	:	89	....			....	
1927	39	47	86	45.35			32,010	
1926	36	47	83	43.37			31,828	

[a] Average number of employees — total man-hours worked, divided by the number of business days.
[b] Devoting most time to selling.
[c] Includes executives.
[d] Some irregularities here — confusion between gross and net transactions, but these make little difference in results.
[e] Net sales and net transactions (?) used, 1932–38.

17. Pay-roll Expenses, as Percentages of Sales, 1924–1940

Year Ending Dec. 31	Administration [a]	Occupancy [b]	Publicity [c]	Buying & Mdsg.[d]	Direct & General Selling [e]	Delivery	Total
1940	3.72	0.54	0.33	2.53	5.57	0.76	13.45
1939	3.69	0.56	0.27	2.53	5.76	0.67	13.48
1938	3.70	0.60	0.26	2.59	5.74	0.71	13.60
1937	3.63	0.48	0.26	2.34	6.04	0.77	13.52
1936	3.48	0.49	0.28	2.25	5.72	0.79	13.01
1935	4.76	0.59	0.33	2.44	5.98	0.78	14.88
1934	4.94	0.59	0.25	2.57	5.82	0.76	14.93
1933	3.91	0.58	0.26	2.44	5.22	0.83	13.24
1932	4.62	0.56	0.23	2.42	5.13	0.85	13.81
1931	3.16	0.47	0.19	2.09	5.07	0.76	11.74
1930	2.96	0.48	0.18	2.02	4.90	0.66	11.20
1929	2.75	0.46	0.17	1.87	4.67	0.60	10.52
1928	2.64	0.31	0.18	1.91	5.48	0.56	11.08
1927	2.75	0.32	0.19	1.88	5.52	0.60	11.26
1926	2.88	0.30	0.21	1.98	5.43	0.63	11.43
1925	...	...	...	...	...	...	....
1924	3.82	0.23	0.30	2.14	4.58	0.79	11.85

[a] Executive, accounting office, accounts receivable and credit, and superintendency.
[b] Operating and housekeeping.
[c] Sales promotion, general advertising, and (in 1940) display.
[d] Buyers and assistants.
[e] Salespeople.

18. CONSTITUTION AND BY-LAWS OF THE ASSOCIATION (UNLIMITED PARTNERSHIP), 1900

In effect prior to the organization of the SOCIETY
into a Massachusetts Corporation, in 1903

CONSTITUTION
November 21, 1900

ARTICLE I. NAME

The name of this SOCIETY shall be the HARVARD CO-OPERATIVE SOCIETY.

ARTICLE II. OBJECT

The object of this SOCIETY shall be to provide suitable arrangements for furnishing books, stationery and other supplies to its members, and members of Harvard University.

ARTICLE III. MEMBERSHIP

The HARVARD CO-OPERATIVE SOCIETY shall consist of all persons connected with Harvard University and Radcliffe College, who shall sign this Constitution, and shall pay an annual fee of one dollar ($1.00). The payment of such fee shall entitle the member to the benefits of the SOCIETY for the fiscal year within which it is paid.

With the approval of the Board of Directors, any alumnus of Harvard, and any member of the Episcopal Theological School, upon payment of one dollar, may receive a ticket that shall entitle him to all privileges of the SOCIETY except the right to vote and hold office.

ARTICLE IV. MEETINGS

There shall be an annual meeting of the SOCIETY on the third Wednesday in November.

The Board of Directors may call other meetings when it sees fit; and it shall be the duty of the President to call a meeting whenever petitioned for by one-tenth of the SOCIETY.

ARTICLE V. OFFICERS

The SOCIETY shall be governed by a Board of Directors, consisting of a President; a Secretary; and eight Directors chosen as follows: one from the Faculty of Arts and Science, one from the Graduate

School, one from the Law School, one from the Medical School, one from the University at large, and one from the Senior, Junior, and Sophomore classes of the College or Scientific School, respectively.

ARTICLE VI. Election of Officers. Tenure

The President, Secretary and other Directors shall be chosen by vote of the Society, at the annual November meeting.

The term of President and of Secretary shall be one year. The term of any other Director shall continue during his connection with that department or class of the University from which he was chosen.

Any vacancy in the Board occurring between the annual November meetings shall be filled until the next annual meeting by a majority vote of the remaining members of the Board.

ARTICLE VII. Duties of Directors

The Board of Directors shall hold regular meetings, and shall keep records of them. The President shall preside at meetings of the Board and of the Society. In his absence, the Board may appoint a President pro tempore.

The Board of Directors shall have all power necessary for the conduct and supervision of the business of the Society. It may delegate the routine management of the business to a Superintendent, whom it shall have the power to appoint and remove.

The Board shall have power to expel from the Society any member whom it may deem unfit for membership; but such expulsion shall require a two-thirds vote of the whole Board.

ARTICLE VIII. Superintendent

The Superintendent shall be appointed and removed by the Board of Directors.

It shall be his duty to conduct the business of the Society in such manner as the Board of Directors shall determine; and he shall give a bond, in such sum as the Board shall fix, for the faithful and honest discharge of his duties. His accounts and vouchers shall at all times be open to the inspection of the Directors.

He shall have authority to engage clerks and assistants, subject to the approval of the Board of Directors.

ARTICLE IX. Division of Profits

The net profits of each year shall be added in part to the capital of the Society, and in part shall be divided among members in such proportion to the purchases made by them as the Board of Directors shall from time to time determine.

ARTICLE X. Dispositions of Capital

In case of the dissolution of the Society or of its cessation from business by voluntary act or otherwise, its net assets shall become the property of the President and Fellows of Harvard College; the income thereof to be used for the embellishment of the College precincts or otherwise at their discretion in such manner as to contribute to the amenity of student life; it being expressly provided, however, that the said President and Fellows shall lend the fund or such part thereof as may seem to them expedient, as capital to any other cooperative society which they may consider properly organized for the benefit of the members of Harvard University.

ARTICLE XI. Amendments

Any article of this Constitution may be amended by a two-thirds vote of the members present and voting at the annual meeting or at any special meeting of the Society called for that purpose.

November 21, 1900.

BY–LAWS

November 21, 1900

I

The fiscal year of the Society shall begin on the First day of July, and end on the Thirtieth day of June.

II

Members shall in no wise transfer their privileges to non-members, nor shall they make purchases on their own tickets in the interest of non-members.

III

Sales made by the Society shall be for cash, except as otherwise provided in this by-law. Officers of instruction in Harvard University shall have the privilege of sales on credit not exceeding one month at any time; and other persons purchasing from the Society shall have the same privilege on filing a bond with the Superintendent, or on depositing cash in such amount as the Board of Directors may from time to time determine.

IV

The bond filed by persons desiring credit under the provisions of By-Law III of the SOCIETY, shall be for not less than two hundred dollars.

The cash deposited by persons desiring such credit shall be not less than fifty dollars.

V

Bills shall be payable not later than the tenth day of the month in which they are presented. If the bills of such as have filed a bond under By-Law III be not paid on the twentieth day of the month, demand may be made on the bondsmen without further notice.

VI

The compensation of the Directors shall be two dollars ($2.00) each for each meeting attended.

VII

Directors absent from two consecutive meetings of the Board, without notice to the Secretary of cause of absence, shall be assumed to have resigned.

November 21, 1900.

19. BY-LAWS OF THE CORPORATION, AS REVISED, 1903–1942

The by-laws, revised April 17, 1942, were adopted at the first meeting of the SOCIETY for the purpose of constituting a corporation to be known as HARVARD CO-OPERATIVE SOCIETY held on the twenty-third day of January, 1903.

Dates of the adoption and the several amendments, together with their references in the volumes and pages of the SOCIETY's Record, are here set forth.

Date		Volume and Page	
January	23, 1903	II	4
May	27, 1904	II	93
October	21, 1904	II	107

November	18, 1904	II	115
October	26, 1905	II	147
October	23, 1908	II	252
October	17, 1913	III	130
November	19, 1915	III	203
June	8, 1916	III	230
August	2, 1917	III	277
September	26, 1917	III	283
October	29, 1919	III	378
October	27, 1920	III	461
November	9, 1921	IV	73
September	25, 1940	VI	405
April	28, 1941	VI	456
April	17, 1942	VII	70

ARTICLE I. NAME AND SEAL

This corporation shall be known by the name of HARVARD CO-OPERATIVE SOCIETY and shall have a corporate seal bearing the inscription: "HARVARD CO-OPERATIVE SOCIETY, Incorporated 1903."

ARTICLE II. OFFICERS AND DIRECTORS

The officers shall be a President, a Vice-President, a Clerk, who may be called Secretary, and a Treasurer, all of whom shall be members of the Board of Directors. Including these officers the Board of Directors shall consist of not more than sixteen members of whom four shall represent the Massachusetts Institute of Technology. The officers and other directors shall be selected as follows: The President, Vice-President, Clerk, and Treasurer from Harvard University or from the Massachusetts Institute of Technology at large; two directors from Harvard University at large; two or more directors from the Massachusetts Institute of Technology at large; one an officer of Harvard University; one from the alumni of Harvard University; one from the student body of the Massachusetts Institute of Technology; one from the Senior class, one from the Junior class and one from the Sophomore class of Harvard College; together with the Manager of the Society, *ex officio*. The term of office of the Vice-President, Treasurer, Clerk and other directors shall be one year. They shall take office on the Saturday following the third Wednesday in November, or on the day following the election of officers by the stockholders. The President shall take office upon his election by the Board of Directors and his term of office shall expire upon the election of his successor.

ARTICLE III. BOARD OF DIRECTORS

The business of the corporation shall be managed by the Board of Directors. The Board of Directors may delegate the routine management of the business to an Executive Committee whom it shall have power to appoint and remove at its pleasure, and to a Manager whom it shall have power to employ upon such terms as to it shall seem proper. No person shall be at once a director and a stockholder.

An Auditing Committee of three Directors shall be chosen at the annual meeting to employ Certified Public Accountants to examine the books and vouchers of the Treasurer and the Manager for the ensuing year and to report thereon to the Auditing Committee for presentation to the Board at the next annual meeting with such recommendations as the Committee shall deem appropriate.

The Board of Directors shall each year make a written or printed report to the stockholders on the state of the SOCIETY, such report to be presented at the annual meeting of the stockholders; and they shall issue a printed report to the participating members of the SOCIETY at least three weeks before the annual meeting of the participating members.

ARTICLE IV. PRESIDENT AND VICE-PRESIDENT

The President shall be the chief executive officer of the corporation and he shall preside, when present, at all meetings of the Board of Directors. He shall be charged with the general oversight, care, and management of all property and business of the corporation in all its departments, and of its agents and servants, except so far as their duties may be specifically prescribed by law, by the By-Laws, or by the Directors. He shall be President of the unincorporated association, the HARVARD CO-OPERATIVE SOCIETY, and shall preside at all its meetings.

The Vice-President, in the absence of the President, shall preside at all meetings of the Board of Directors and shall perform the other functions herein prescribed for the President.

ARTICLE V. Clerk

The Clerk shall be sworn to the faithful performance of his duties before entering upon the performance thereof. He shall attend all meetings of the stockholders and directors, and shall keep a record of their votes and of all business transacted at said meetings. He shall give notice of the meetings of the stockholders in accordance with provisions of Article VIII, and, at the request of the President or of a majority of the directors, of meetings of the Board of Directors.

ARTICLE VI. Treasurer

The Treasurer shall have oversight and direction of all receipts and all disbursements of the corporation. He shall have oversight and direction over all moneys and all books of account of the corporation. He shall sign all certificates of stock, and he shall keep the stock-book and stock-ledger.

ARTICLE VII. Manager

It shall be the duty of the Manager to conduct the business of the Society in such a manner as the Board of Directors shall determine; and he shall give a bond, with a surety or sureties satisfactory to the Board of Directors, in such sum as the Board shall fix, for the faithful and honest discharge of his duties. His accounts and vouchers shall at all times be open to the inspection of the directors and to the stockholders.

He shall have authority to engage clerks and assistants, but if, in the opinion of the majority of the Board of Directors, any clerk or assistant shall seem incompetent or otherwise unfit for the duties assigned him, the Board of Directors may require the Manager to discharge such clerk or assistant.

He shall attend all meetings of the Board of Directors and make thereat such reports on the Society's business as the directors may require. He shall submit to the directors for their approval at the beginning of each fiscal year an expense budget for the fiscal year ensuing. He shall be responsible that no payments on expense account are without a prior appropriation therefor. He shall have general charge of the system of central merchandise control and shall perform such other functions as the Board of Directors may from time to time assign to him.

ARTICLE VIII. Meetings of Stockholders *

At the annual meeting a majority of the stockholders in person shall be a quorum. At other meetings three stockholders in person shall constitute a quorum.

The annual meeting of stockholders shall be held on the last Wednesday in September, in each year, and a second meeting for the purpose of electing the directors and officers shall be held on the last Wednesday in October.

Notice of the annual meeting, stating place and hour, shall be mailed by the clerk to each stockholder at his address as the same appears upon the records of the Society, at least seven days prior to the meeting.

At such annual meeting, if a majority of the stockholders shall not be represented, the stockholders present shall have power to adjourn to a day certain, and notice of the time and place to which the meeting has been adjourned shall be given by the Clerk depositing in the mail at least five days before the day set for such adjourned meeting, exclusive of the day of mailing, a copy of the notice of such meeting addressed to each stockholder; but if a majority of the stockholders be present in person, the stockholders so present shall have power, from time to time, to adjourn the annual meeting to any subsequent day or days, and no notice of the adjourned meeting need be given.

Special meetings of the stockholders shall at the request of the Board of Directors, or upon the petition of not less than fifty holders of participating tickets, be called by the Clerk by a notice stating the place, day, hour, and purposes of such meeting, mailed at least two days prior to the date of meeting, to each stockholder of record at his address, as it appears on the records of the Society.

In the absence of the President or the Vice-President, the stockholders shall elect a President *pro tempore,* and in the absence of the Clerk the stockholders shall elect a Clerk *pro tempore.*

---

* The capital stock of the Harvard Co-operative Society (Incorporated) is held by ten stockholders, in accordance with the provisions of Chapter 447 of the Acts of 1913 and acts in amendment thereof. The stock is held subject to trust provisions and to the terms of these By-Laws. Stockholders serve for five-year terms and are chosen by the remaining stockholders.

ARTICLE IX. Meetings of Directors

Stated meetings of the directors shall be held, without notice, on some day certain for each month, to be set by the directors, except June, July, August, and September. The day, hour, and place of meeting shall be set by vote of the Board.

Special meetings of the Board may be called by the President, or by the Clerk at the written request of a majority of the Board of Directors, on notice, mailed, telegraphed, or delivered to each director; but in June, July, August, and September one week's notice must be given. During June, July, August, and September, or during any period in which the United States shall be at war and for six months after the cessation of the hostilities thereof, five directors may constitute a quorum to do business.

ARTICLE X. Nominations

The stockholders shall nominate at their annual meeting in September, a President, a Vice-President, a Treasurer, and a Clerk from the University or from the Massachusetts Institute of Technology at large, and the other directors to be selected as follows: Two directors from Harvard University at large; two or more directors from the Massachusetts Institute of Technology at large; an officer of Harvard University; one from the alumni of Harvard University; one from the student body of the Massachusetts Institute of Technology; one from the Senior class, one from the Junior class, and one from the Sophomore class of Harvard College. These nominations shall be posted in the Society's store and published in the *Crimson* and *The Tech*, or in such college publications as are designated by the stockholders, two weeks before the annual meeting of the participating members of the Society. Other nominations, if any, shall be made by nomination papers signed by twenty-five participating members of the Society, such nomination papers to be delivered to the Clerk of the corporation at least eight days before the meeting. It shall be the duty of the Clerk to post and publish all nomination papers. If additional nominations are made in this manner, the President, Vice-President, Treasurer, Clerk, and other directors shall be selected by ballot at the annual meeting of the participating members, provided that at least ten per centum of the participating members who have the right to vote are present and are voting. No stockholder shall be nominated for any office in this corporation.

ARTICLE XI. Elections

The persons so elected by ballot, or, if no additional nominations are made or if less than ten per centum of the participating members who have the right to vote are present and are voting at the annual meeting of the ticket-holders, the nominees of the stockholders, shall be elected by the stockholders. The director nominated for President, as provided in Article X, shall be elected by the Board of Directors at their first meeting. New stockholders, to fill vacancies caused by lapse of time, death, or resignation, shall be selected in the same manner and at the same time as the Vice-President, Treasurer, Clerk, and directors.

Any vacancy in the Board of Directors may be filled by the remaining directors until the annual meeting next ensuing. Any officer may resign by filing his resignation with the Clerk. Any stockholder may retire from his position in the same manner, upon surrender of his certificate of stock. The remaining stockholders may fill this vacancy until the annual meeting next ensuing.

ARTICLE XII. Business

The present mode of conducting the business and the present scope of the dealings shall not be altered by this corporation without express vote of the directors, and as then fixed, shall not be again altered without express vote.

ARTICLE XIII. Contracts

The stockholders shall determine what compensation, if any, shall be received by the President, Vice-President, Treasurer, Clerk, or any member of the Board of Directors.

Sealed instruments shall be sealed with the corporate seal and executed by the President and Treasurer. Notes shall be signed by the Treasurer in person. Checks may be signed by the Treasurer in person, or by such other person or persons as he shall authorize. Checks and notes shall be upon numbered blanks.

ARTICLE XIV. Participating Tickets

A participating ticket shall be issued to each officer or student or past member of Harvard University, Radcliffe College, or the Episcopal Theological School, and such other persons or corporations as the directors shall vote, who shall pay to the Society an annual fee of one dollar, and who shall agree in writing to be bound by the By-Laws and regulations of the Society. The payment, agreement, and issue of a ticket in accordance with the foregoing provision, shall entitle the holder of the ticket, for the period of the current fiscal year, to the right to trade at the stores of the Society and with affiliated concerns, and to participate in the annual distribution of the profits of the Society. The ticket-holders shall constitute the unincorporated association, the Harvard Co-operative Society.

Of the said ticket-holders, those who are officers or students in Harvard University alone shall have the right to vote at the meetings of the Harvard Co-operative Society (the unincorporated association), as designated in the By-Laws of that association.

The annual meeting of the participating members of the said association, contemplated by the By-Laws of this corporation, shall be held on the third Wednesday of October.

ARTICLE XV. Division of Profits

The directors of this corporation shall, in accordance with votes, conforming with the provisions of Chapter 447 of the Acts of 1913 and Acts in amendment thereof, passed by the stockholders from time to time, apportion, following the instructions as given them, the earnings of this corporation. The power to give instructions as to such apportionment shall be vested in the stockholders in their discretion by virtue hereof; but any dividends declared upon the stock held by them shall be devoted to the payment for further stock of the corporation or turned into its treasury as addition to the surplus thereof.

ARTICLE XVI. Dissolution

The ten stockholders shall have the right to apply at any time to the Court for a dissolution of the corporation, and upon its legal dissolution all assets of the corporation shall vest, subject to its liabilities, in the general body of participating members, as a voluntary association, of the same nature and with the same Constitution and By-Laws as those of the present Society at the moment before this incorporation.

ARTICLE XVII. AMENDMENT

The stockholders may make any change in these By-Laws by a majority vote at any regularly called meeting at which a majority of the stockholders are present, except that no change may be made in this manner which shall alter the relations subsisting between this corporation, the HARVARD CO-OPERATIVE SOCIETY, and the unincorporated society, the HARVARD CO-OPERATIVE SOCIETY.

Any such change must take place by the mutual consent of the stockholders and the participating members of the SOCIETY. The assent of the members shall be manifested by a majority vote in favor of any proposed change, provided that the votes represent twenty-five per cent of the members of the SOCIETY. The vote shall be by Australian ballot, after at least two weeks' notice of the subject of the balloting. Such notice, however, shall be given only at the joint request of a majority of the stockholders and fifty members of the SOCIETY.

INDEX

INDEX

Academic costume, 131–132
Academic customers, 110. *See also* Members
Accounting procedure, 25, 34–40. *See also* Cost accounting; Financial policy
Accounting courses, 39
Addition of lines, 113–114. *See also* Diversification
Administration, 6–7, 23, 32, 34, 37, 44–83, 86–92, 115–119, 123, 133, 141, 158–159;
cost of, 167. *See also* Board of Directors
Advantages in Membership, 7, 139–142. *See also* Dividends; Services
Advertising, 109, 111. *See also* College papers; Publicity
Affiliated stores, 7, 11, 21, 112–113, 121, 134, 142
Alumni, relations with H. C. S., 29, 63, 98, 109–110, 151–152
Amee and Waterman, 22
Amendments to constitution, 7
Ames, James B., 17, 20, 22, 24–25, 41, 47, 51, 94, 145
Annual reports, 65, 80
Assets and liabilities, 24, 82, 93, 116. *See also* Accounting
Assistant managers of departments, 165
Attendance at meetings, 47, 70, 116, 136–137
Auditor's reports, 38, 40, 117
Automobiles and automotive supplies, 113, 134
Average
attendance at meetings, 136;
dividends, 134;
number of employees, classified, 166
Ayres, Charles H., 55, 145, 148

Balance sheets, 36
Baldwin, William H., 146

Ballantine, Arthur A., 53, 55, 64, 145–146
Bank holiday, 101, 113
Banking services, 54, 101, 132, 142
Barbershop at School of Business, 160–163;
Technology, 160–163
Blackwell, H. L., 64, 148
Board of Directors, 23, 85–88, 147–149;
alumni member, 63–64;
attendance at meetings, 34, 116, 171;
committees of, 31–32, 34, 37, 44, 63, 117;
control by, 6, 47, 50–53, 59, 117, 169, 173;
election of, 6, 51, 168–169;
fees to, 44, 59, 69, 171;
Minutes of, 22–23;
relations with manager, 27–43, 62–63, 85;
reports, 36;
tenure of office, 169
Bolles, Frank, 7, 49, 65, 145, 147
Bond issue, 116
Bond requirements, 141
Bonuses, 22, 30, 68–69
Books,
department of, 31, 56, 106, 133, 165;
discounts on, 11;
monopolistic control of, 20;
problems in handling, 15, 20, 22;
second-hand, 10;
titles, 133. *See also* Law books; Textbooks
Borrowing, 119. *See also* Financing; Mortgage
Boston *Advertiser*, 9
Boston Elevated Company, 72
Branches of H. C. S., 72–77. *See also* specific branches
Bryn Mawr College, 127
Buildings, 11, 35, 53–59, 94–96
Bull Moose campaign, 48
Bullock, C. J., 115

Business cycles, 16–17, 23, 92–93. *See also* Depressions
Business done by H. C. S., *see* Volume of business
Buying
expense, 158, 167;
habits, 4–7
By-laws, 91, 170–179

Cambridge Trust Company, 81, 119
Capital, 17, 36, 81–82, 153–155, 170. *See also* Financing; Surplus
Cash sales, 7, 129, 160–163. *See also* Dividends; Volume of business
Chain stores, competition of, 120, 130
Chapman, Henry G., Jr., 146
Charge sales, 141, 159–163
Check-cashing by H. C. S., 132, 142
Claims for damages, 77–78
Clark, Grenville, 55
Classes of membership of H. C. S., 122, 151–152, 164
Classification of H. C. S. customers, 110, 139–140, 152, 164. *See also* Members
Clerk of H. C. S., 174
Cole, Edwin T., 74, 148
Cole, George E., vi, 67, 70, 84–86, 94, 142, 146
Cole, William Morse, 39–40
College House, 10–11
College papers, 8, 33, 51, 111. *See also* specific publications
Colonial Club, 54, 69
Comey, E. H., 96
Competition, 101–102, 112, 120, 130
Constitution, 6–7, 123, 140, 168–170
Contract-pressing business, 131
Control, 27–43. *See also* Administration; Management; Stock control
Controller's office, v
Coolidge, Archibald C., 40
"Coop number," use of in purchasing, 104–105
Co-operative societies, 3, 5, 73, 113, 125–129, 132;
in Great Britain, 5, 22. *See also* Harvard Co-operative Society
Cornell University, 126–127

Cost accounting, 34–40, 67, 107–111
Cost of doing business, 107–111, 120, 156–157
Cost of living, 4, 29
Cost of sales, 156–157
Counsel, 64, 87, 141
Credits and collections, 4, 68, 114, 129. *See also* Charge sales
Crimson, v, 4, 23–24, 48, 50, 137
Criticisms, 24, 49, 86–92, 98, 119–124, 128, 138, 140
Cummings, Edward, 145, 147
Curtis, Allen, 145
Cutler, William W., 145, 147
Customers, vi, 110. *See also* Classification of H. C. S. customers
Cutlery, 95

Dane Hall, 11, 35, 57, 59
Dartmouth College, 125–127
David, Donald K., vii, 85, 149
Davis, Frances, 102
Debts, bad, 109. *See also* Credits and collections
Definition of co-operative societies, 140
Delivery, 114;
equipment, 45, 113;
expense, 158, 167;
number of employees, 165
Democracy in H. C. S., *see* Undemocratic control
Departmentalization, 31–33, 133, 141. *See also* specific departments
Deposit requirements, 141
Depreciation, 37, 45, 68, 77, 79, 81, 158
Depressions, 113. *See also* Business cycles
Description of stores,
main, 94–96;
School of Business, 99–100;
Technology, 97–98
Dewey, Davis R., 89, 150
Directors of H. C. S., *see* Board of Directors
Discontinuance of lines, 16, 45, 114, 130–131
Discounts paid by affiliated stores, 7, 11, 21, 112–113, 121
Dissolution, provisions for, 178

Diversification, 31, 66, 113–114, 119
Dividends,
  amount, 28, 59;
  on charge sales, 141, 159–163;
  policy, 7, 21, 68, 75, 90, 117, 127, 141, 169, 178;
  rates, 28, 59, 79–81, 93, 120, 129, 134–135, 153–155, 159
Division of profits, see Dividends; Profit-sharing
Donham, Wallace B., vii, 89, 99, 150
Downey, O. J., 96
Drury's tobacco shop, 11
Dues, 6, 21, 27, 153–155, 168
Dunbar, Charles F., 3

Early difficulties, 3–26
Education in co-operation, 136–138
Effect of general business, 16–17, 23, 28, 79, 117
Elections, 6, 51, 89–90, 139, 168–169, 177
Electrical appliances, 95, 113
Eliot, Charles W., 3, 9, 31, 40, 147
Employees,
  bonuses, 22, 30, 68–69;
  classification by departments, 165;
  compensation, 12, 22, 30, 56, 70, 72, 85, 102–106, 109, 141, 158;
  group insurance, 105;
  interviewed, vi;
  number, 103, 165–166;
  pension, 105;
  training, 25, 104
Employees' Reserve Fund, 69
England, co-operative associations in, 5, 22
Episcopal Theological Seminary, 110, 140, 152
Executive committee, 34, 63
Exemption from taxes, 121
Extra sales people, 103

Faculty membership, 7, 50, 109, 145–152
Field, James A., 146
Financial capitalism, 49, 118
Financial-industrial capitalism, 118–120

Financial policy, 6, 17, 28, 81–82, 170. See also Capital; Dividend policy; Financing
Financing, 6, 16–18, 22, 28, 36, 56, 60, 81, 101, 115–119, 153–155. See also Accounting
Fire, 77–78
Fiske, Charles H., 145
Fluctuations in business, effect upon H. C. S., 16–17, 23, 28, 79, 117
Ford, Horace S., 117, 146, 149
Ford Motor Company, 118
Forgery, 56
Founding, 3–26
Fountain pens, 26, 95, 111
Frankfurter, Felix, 89, 150
Free services, 132, 142
"Freezing," 114
Fuel sales, 12, 54, 56, 114, 131
Furber, George P., 146
Furniture, 12, 95;
  free storage, 12;
  second-hand, 6–7, 15, 131
Future problems, 119–124

Gardiner, John H., 146, 148
Gay, Edwin F., 40, 54, 64, 84, 89, 150
Goodwill, 46
Goodwin, M. H., 70–71, 146, 148
Government control, 38, 87, 112, 114
Gray, John H., 146
Greenough, Chester N., 89, 150
Groceries, 45, 66
Group insurance, 105
Growth, 61–83. See also Volume of business

Hale, Herbert D., 145
Hardware, 130
Hart, Albert Bushnell, 41, 48, 147
Harvard Bureau of Business Research, vi, 107–108
Harvard Co-operative Society,
  accounting procedure, 25, 34–40;
  administration, 6–7, 23, 32–34, 37, 44–83, 86–92, 115–119, 123, 133, 141, 158–159, 167;
  affiliated stores, 7, 11, 21, 112–113, 121, 134, 142;

annual reports, 65, 80;
as partnership, 124, 139;
as purchasing agent for University, 66, 108, 130;
assets (*see also* investments) and liabilities, 24, 82, 93, 116;
auditor's reports, 38, 40;
banking services, 54, 101, 132, 142;
bond issue, 116;
bond requirements, 171;
bonuses, 22, 30, 68–69;
budget, 107;
buildings, 11, 35, 53–59, 94–96;
by-laws, 124;
capital, 17, 36, 81–82, 153–155, 170;
cash sales, 7, 129, 160–163;
claims for damages, 77–78;
competition, 101–102, 112, 120, 130;
constitution, 6–7, 123, 140, 168–170;
cost accounting, 34–40, 67, 107–111;
cost of doing business, 107–111, 120, 156–157;
counsel, 64, 87, 141;
credit policy, 68, 114, 129;
criticisms of, 24, 49, 86–92, 98, 119–124, 128, 138, 140;
deficit, 16;
delivery, 45, 113, 158;
departmentalization, 31–33, 133, 141;
depreciation policy, 37, 45, 68, 77, 79, 81, 158;
discontinuance of lines, 16, 45, 114, 130–131;
discounts, 11, 54;
dissolution, provisions for, 178;
diversification, 31, 66, 113–114, 119;
dividend policy, 7, 21, 68, 75, 90, 117, 127, 141, 169, 178;
dividend rates, 28, 59, 79–81, 93, 120, 129, 134–135, 153–155, 159;
dues, 6, 21, 27, 153–155, 168;
early difficulties, 3–26;
educational activities, 138;
effect of general business upon, 16–17, 23, 28, 79, 117;
effect of war upon, 79, 96, 100, 114;
elections, 6, 51, 89–90, 139, 168–169, 177;
employee benefits, 68–69, 105;

executive committee, 34, 63;
financial policy, 6, 17, 28, 81–82, 170;
financing, 6, 16–18, 22, 28, 36, 56, 60, 81, 101, 115–119, 153–155;
fire at, 77–78;
forgery at, 56;
founding, 3–26;
free services, 132;
future problems, 119–124;
government control, 38, 87, 112, 114;
growth, 61–83;
incorporation, 47–60, 129, 139;
influence of (*see also* price levels), 125–130;
inventory control, 24, 84, 96, 114;
investments, real estate, 18, 53, 56–57, 129, 155, 158;
labor difficulties, 104, 106;
leased departments, 130;
liabilities, 24, 82;
location, 9–11;
losses, 55–56;
mail-order business, 66, 130;
maintenance force, 165;
management and control, 10–12, 16–18, 23–43, 57, 60, 67, 84–124;
market analysis, 121;
monopolistic features, 20;
mortgage, 57, 81, 116;
net gain, 12, 153–157;
nominations, 23, 89–90, 176;
occupancy expense (*see also* investments; rent), 158–159, 167;
officers (*see also* specific persons), 168–169, 172–173;
operating data, 153–167;
organization, 6–9, 31–33, 64, 133, 141;
overages, 67;
planning, 61–83;
policy-formulation, 6–7, 18–23, 44–60, 65–70, 82, 90, 94, 112;
preferred-stock issue, 81–82;
price levels, 4, 12, 15, 17, 20, 59, 94, 134, 142;
price policy, 12, 15, 17, 20, 87, 94, 112, 120;
profit policy, 7, 54, 58–59, 86, 120;
profit-sharing, 23, 29–31, 42–43, 60;

prosperity, 15, 22–23, 27–28, 60, 92–94;
publicity, 8, 109, 111, 158, 167;
purchasing costs, 158, 167;
purchasing policy, 11, 20, 45, 66, 108;
purposes, 58–59, 168;
relations with alumni, 29, 63, 98, 109–110, 151–152; banks, 81, 119; public, 19, 125–129;
rent, 11, 57;
reorganization, 44–60;
repairs, 158;
reserves, 93;
salaries paid, 12, 22, 30, 56, 70, 72, 85, 102–106, 109, 141, 158;
sales policy, 7, 19, 65, 138, 140, 170;
sales promotion, 109;
second-hand goods, 6–7, 15, 131;
services, 31, 73, 98, 120, 131–134, 158;
shortages, 38–42, 56, 67;
stages in history of, 118–119;
stock control, 65, 67, 79, 174;
storage facilities, 12, 96;
surplus, 6, 16, 28, 36, 60, 116, 129, 153–155;
taxes, 121, 158;
theft at, 41, 56–57, 108;
training of staff, 25, 104;
trustees, 50–53, 90;
volume of business, 12, 15, 18, 27, 73, 92, 99–100, 129, 134, 153–155, 160–163. See also Board of Directors; Branches; Employees; Meetings; Members; Reports; Salesforce; Stockholders; specific departments and persons
Harvard Daily Echo, 3, 8–9
Harvard Graduate School of Business Administration, 31, 40, 54, 64, 99–100. See also School of Business Store
Harvard Law School, 7, 17, 54
Harvard Square, 57, 77, 120; Business Men's Association, 54; monopoly in, 5; prices in, 4–5, 94
Harvard Trust Company, 119
Harvard Union, 51, 115

Harvard University, 3, 88, 125; accounting courses, 39; cost of living at, 4; purchasing policy, 66, 108, 130–131; tuition cost, 4
Haskins, Charles H., 90, 150
Hatfield, H. R., 40
Herald, 4
Higginson, Henry L., 51, 149
Hiring of employees, 139
Holyoke House, 11
House furnishings, 165
Hughes, C. W., 100
Humphreys, Walter, vi, 64, 74, 146, 148

Income, 153–157. See also Volume of business
Incorporation, 47–60, 129, 139
Increase in assets, 116; cost of doing business, 109, 111; dividends, 27–28; employees, 103, 165; membership, 27, 92, 151–152; salaries, 72, 167; sales, 28–29, 92–93, 153–155, 160–163; stock, 32
Industrial capitalism, 52, 83, 118, 120
Influence of H. C. S. upon other co-operatives, 125–130; prices, 12, 15, 17, 20, 59, 94, 134, 142
Installment sales, 160–163
Inventory control, 24, 84, 96, 114
Investments in real estate, 18, 53, 56–57, 129, 155, 158

Jobbers, 108
Johnson, Arthur H., 63
Johnson, Lewis J., 145
Johnson, Shirley E., 146

King's, Moses, Bookstore, 15
Kip, Charles Hayden, 3–15, 49, 65, 94, 115, 145
Knox, Mrs., 133
Kruskal, W. H., 137

Labor difficulties, 104
Lamont, Thomas W., 145, 147
Lampoon, 4
Langdell, Christopher Columbus, 3
Lanman, Charles R., 7, 11, 145, 147
Laundry services, 131
Law books, 15, 54–55, 66, 130
Laws, Frederick A., 53–56, 70, 146, 148
Leased department, 130
Leighton, Delmar, 87, 149
Liabilities, 24, 82
Life insurance, group, 105
Loans, 16–18, 119. *See also* Financing; Mortgage
Local dealers, 4–5, 57, 77, 94, 120. *See also* Competition
Location, 9–11. *See also* Branches
Losses, 55–56
Lowell, A. Lawrence, 89, 150
Lowell, James Russell, 3
Luggage transfer, 132
Lyceum Hall, 35, 57, 77
Lyford, Charles D., 27, 29–30, 34, 36, 40–42, 146

Maclachlan, A. D., 74
Maclaurin, R. C., 74
Macy, R. H., and Co., Inc., 112, 118
Mail-order business, 66, 130
Main store, 94–97, 141, 160–165. *See also* Harvard Co-operative Society
Making a purchase at H. C. S., 104–105
Management, 10–12, 23–43, 57, 60, 67, 84–124;
  changes in, 106–115;
  financial, 16–18, 28, 36, 60, 81, 115–119
Manager, 6, 84–124. *See also* Superintendents
Managers of departments, number of, 165
Managing director, 62, 146. *See also* Manager; Superintendents
Mark, Edward L., 146
Massachusetts Institute of Technology, 59, 88, 123, 137, 140, 152. *See also* Technology Store
McInnes, William M., 82, 146

Medical School Branch, 32, 66, 72;
  discontinuance of, 46, 130;
  inventory, 32, 46;
  manager, 44–46;
  profit-sharing, 44;
  salaries, 44
Meetings, 50, 139. *See also* Attendance at meetings; Board of Directors
Members, 17;
  alumni, 151–152;
  as investing capitalists, 135;
  classification, 19, 110, 139–140, 151–152, 164;
  liability of, 47, 60;
  meetings of, 50, 139;
  number, 27, 129, 164;
  students, 9, 151–152;
  teachers, 151–152
Memorial Hall Dining Association, 4
Men's furnishings, 31–32, 40, 54, 56, 165
Merchandise control, 67, 174. *See also* Stock control
Meyer, Hugo R., 146
Minutes of Directors, v, 22–23
Monopolistic features, 20
Moriarty, H. C., 106
Mortgage, 57, 81, 116
Mott, Luther W., 146, 148
Munro, William B., 53, 61–85, 88, 94, 136, 145–146, 148, 150
Murdock, Kenneth B., 88, 149

National Association of College Stores, 128
National Association of Wool Manufacturers, 86, 88
National capitalism, 118
National Committee on Student Co-operatives, 128
N.R.A., 111, 114
Net gain, 12, 153–157
New Deal, 93, 111
Newspaper publicity, 8–9. *See also* College papers
Nominations, 23, 89–90, 176
Non-academic customers, 19, 29, 92, 110, 140. *See also* Members
Non-dividend sales, 121

Non-selling force, 103, 166
Norton, Charles Eliot, 3
Notary services, 132, 142
Number of
department managers, 165;
directors, 7;
employees, 103, 165–166;
members, 27, 129, 164;
sales transactions, 166;
stockholders, 89–90

Occupancy expense, 158–159, 167. See also Investments in real estate; Rent
Officers of H. C. S., vi, 6, 51, 141, 145–150, 168–169, 172–173. See also specific officers
Old Colony Trust Company, 119
Operating data, 153–167
Optical department, 45, 113
Organization, 6–9, 31–33, 64, 133, 141
Osborne, Thomas M., 146
Overages, 67
Ownership of property by H. C. S., 18, 53, 56–57, 129, 155, 158

Paint, 130
Participating members, see Ticket-holders
Partnership, 124, 139
Patronage dividends, see Dividends
Pay-roll expense of H. C. S., as percentage of sales, 167. See also Salaries
Pension, 105
Percentage of
expense to sales, 156–158;
membership in branches to total, 97, 100;
non-dividend to total sales, 121;
pay roll to sales, 167
Periodicals, 8–9. See also College papers
Petty capitalists, 25, 82, 118, 120
Planning, 61–83
Plattsburgh,
H. C. S. branch in, 72–73
Policies, see Credits and collections; Depreciation; Dividend policy; Financial policy; Policy-formula-tion; Profit policy; Purchasing policy; Sales policy
Policy-formulation, 6–7, 18–23, 28, 34, 44–60, 65–70, 82, 90, 94, 112. See also Board of Directors; specific officers
Preferred-stock issue, 81–82
Presidents of H. C. S., 6, 11, 17, 22, 24, 33–34, 55, 61–83, 90, 115–119, 145, 173;
salary, 44, 59
Pressing, 131
Price levels, 79;
as affected by H. C. S., 12, 15, 17, 20, 59, 94, 134, 142;
in Harvard Square, 4, 134
Price policy, 12, 15, 17, 20, 87, 94, 112, 120
Princeton University, 3, 126–127
Professors in H. C. S., 50, 109, 145–152. See also individual professors
Profit policy, 7, 54, 58–59, 86, 120
Profit-sharing, 23, 29–31, 42–43, 60
Profits, distribution of, see Dividends; Profit-sharing
Prosperity, 15, 22–23, 27–28, 60, 92–94. See also Dividends; Profits; Volume of business
Public, relations with, 19, 125–129
Publicity, 8, 109, 111, 158, 167
Purchasing costs, 158, 167
Purchasing policy, 11, 20, 45, 66, 108
Purposes of H. C. S., 58–59, 168

Quincy, Josiah, 7, 147

Radcliffe College, 66, 89, 110, 140, 152
Radio department, 95
Rate of dividends, see Dividends
Ready-to-wear clothing, 96, 165. See also Men's furnishings
Real-estate ownership, expense of, see Investments; Mortgage; Rent
Records,
preservation of, vi, 96;
stock, 45
Redfield, A. C., 87
Relations with
alumni, 29, 63, 98, 109–110, 151–152;
banks, 81, 119;

government, 38, 87, 112, 114; public, 19, 125–129. *See also* Employees
Rent, 11, 57
Reorganization, 44–60
Reports of
  auditor, 38, 40, 117;
  president, 65;
  superintendent, 23, 35;
  treasurer, 12, 81, 116, 136, 174
Reserves, 93. *See also* Depreciation
Retirement of H. C. S. employees, 105
Rice, Carl, 98
Rochdale Pioneers, 5, 22
Rogers, Robert E., 102

Sabine, Wallace C., 89
Salaries, 12, 22, 30, 56, 70, 72, 85, 102–106, 109, 141, 158
Sales,
  cash, 7, 129, 160–163;
  charge, 141, 159–163;
  cost, 156–157;
  installment, 160–163;
  number per employee, 166. *See also* Volume of business
Salesforce, 30, 68–69, 102–106, 165–166
Sales policy, 7, 19, 65, 138, 140, 170
Schaub, Lincoln F., 64, 87, 145, 148
School of Business Store,
  barbershop, 160–163;
  classification of sales, 121;
  description, 99–100;
  employees, 165;
  financing, 101;
  members, 164;
  volume of business, 97, 100–163
Scott, Austin W., vi, 87, 112, 142, 145, 149–150
Sears, Roebuck and Co., 120
Second-hand goods, 6–7, 15, 131
Secretaries of H. C. S., 25, 55, 86, 145–146;
  duties, 33, 62–63, 90;
  fees to, 44, 59
Secretary-treasurer of H. C. S., 41, 45
Selling-policy of H. C. S., 7, 19, 65, 138, 140, 170
Services, 31, 73, 98, 120, 131–134, 142, 158

Sever's, Charles W., University Bookstore, 15
Sherman Anti-trust Act, 58
Shoe-repairing, 32
Shortages, 38–42, 56, 67. *See also* Theft
Smith, J. A., 67
Smokers' supplies, 11, 54, 66
Solicitors, 101–102
Sport goods, 95, 111, 113–114, 165
Stages in H. C. S. history, 118–119
Stanford University, 127
State regulation, 38
Stationery and stationers' supplies, 11, 31–32, 72–73, 95, 165
Statistics, 21, 27–30, 32, 35–37, 40, 72, 79, 81, 89, 92–94, 97, 99–100, 103, 109, 111, 116, 121, 129, 134–137, 145–167. *See also* Members; Profits; Volume of business
Stock,
  control of, 65, 67, 79, 174;
  records, 45;
  theft of, 41, 56–57, 108
Stock records, 45
Stockholders of H. C. S., 32–33, 52, 86, 89–92, 122, 139, 149–150, 175
Storage facilities, 96
Strikes, 104
Student aid, 9
Students
  as founders of H. C. S., 3–26;
  as participators in administration, 13, 41, 48–49;
  as members, 9, 29, 151–152
Subway, 72
Success, 15, 22–23, 27–28, 60, 92–94. *See also* Dividends
Sullavan, Margaret, 102
Sullivan, M. A., 47–49, 148
Superintendents, 6, 8, 10–12, 16, 22–26, 70–72, 146;
  control of, 23, 27–43, 45, 57, 62–63, 85, 169;
  salaries of, 56, 70, 72, 85, 141;
  selection of, 10, 27, 139. *See also* Manager
Surplus, 6, 16, 28, 36, 60, 116, 129, 153–155
Swift and Company, 118

Tailoring department, 31–32, 57, 66, 78, 96, 104, 130, 165

Taussig, Frank W., 17, 20, 23, 25, 28–31, 33–34, 36, 38–40, 47, 55, 145, 147

Taxes, 121, 158

Taylor, John L., 67, 82, 146

Technology Barbershop, 75, 97; volume of sales (cash, charge, and installment), 160–163

Technology Co-operative Society, 74

Technology Lunch, 97–98; volume of sales (cash, charge, and installment), 160–163

Technology Store, 72–77, 102; dividend policy, 159; members, classified by purchases, 164; number of employees, 165; percentage of non-dividend sales, 121; percentage of total sales, membership, and employees, 97, 99; volume of sales, 160–163. *See also* Technology Barbershop; Technology Lunch

Tennis equipment, 11

Tenure of office, 89, 169

Textbooks, 7, 15, 130. *See also* Books; Law books

Theater-ticket sales, 109

Theft, 41, 56–57, 108

Thomas, F. H., 44–46

Thompson, Henry S., vi, 63, 83, 85–86, 115–119, 145, 148

Thurston's stationery store, 66, 72–73

Ticket-holders, 48, 50, 177–178. *See also* Members

Tickets, members', 104–105, 177–178; theater, 109; travel, 130

Tobacco, 54. *See also* Smokers' supplies

Toys, 95

Track Fund loan, 16

Training of staff, 25, 104

Transactions, number of, 166–167

Travel bureau, 130

Treasurers of H. C. S., 63, 90, 117, 146; duties, 174; election, 6; reports of, 12, 81, 116, 136, 174; salary of, 59

Trustees, 50–53, 90

Undemocratic control, 49, 86–92, 123, 128, 138

Unionization, 103–104

University of Louisiana, 127

University of Michigan, 125–126

University of Minnesota, 127

University of Texas, 127

University of Toronto, 5, 73, 126

Variations among co-operatives, 125–130

Vice-presidents of H. C. S., 64, 87, 141, 145, 173

Volume of business, 12, 15, 18, 27, 73, 92, 99–100, 129, 134, 153–155, 160–163

Wall Street, 119–120

Wambaugh, Eugene, 28, 34, 145, 148

War, effect of, 79, 96, 100, 114

Warehouse, 96

Waterman, A. A., and Company, 22

Waterman, Arthur A., 8, 10–12, 16, 22–26, 115, 146–147

Weaver, W. E., 41, 45, 49, 146

Westengard, Jens I., 47, 148

White, John W., 11, 13, 145

Wilson, Carroll L., 88, 149

Winsor, Justin, 3

Women as H. C. S. employees, 105–106

Women's wares, 94

Wood, May J., 106

Woodworth, A. V., 25, 145

World Wars, effect upon H. C. S., 79, 96, 100, 114

Woolworth, F. W., Co., 120

Wyman, Bruce, 51, 150

Yale University, 113, 125–127, 132